INTENTIONAL
ministry
in a not-so-mega church

BECOMING A MISSIONAL COMMUNITY

Dennis Bickers

BEACON HILL PRESS
OF KANSAS CITY

Cover Design: Brandon Hill
Interior Design: Sharon Page

Unless otherwise indicated, all Scripture quotations are from the *New King James Version* (NKJV). Copyright © 1979, 1980, 1982 by Thomas Nelson, Inc. Used by permission. All rights reserved.

Library of Congress Cataloging-in-Publication Data

Bickers, Dennis W., 1948-
    Intentional ministry in a not-so-mega church : becoming a missional community / Dennis Bickers.
        p. cm.
    Includes bibliographical references (p.   ).
    ISBN 978-0-8341-2434-9 (pbk.)
    1. Small churches. 2. Church growth. 3. Mission of the church. I. Title.

    BV637.8.B533 2009
    253—dc22

2008049945

10 9 8 7 6 5 4 3 2 1

DEDICATION

I had the distinct pleasure of serving as pastor to only one church for twenty years. In 1981 I began my pastorate at Hebron Baptist Church near Madison, Indiana. The church was struggling to survive, and yet they were willing to take a chance with a young man who had no education beyond high school and no experience as a pastor. Maybe they thought they had nothing to lose, but few churches would have given me the opportunity they gave me.

They allowed me the opportunity to grow and develop as a minister. They loved me and my family. In time, they accepted my leadership and dared to do things they had never done before. It was a time of tremendous transition, and we made many mistakes along the way. We also enjoyed some amazing victories. The victories helped us overcome the mistakes and continue to do ministry together. It was an exciting two decades, and those years continue to impact my life and ministry today. Hebron taught me the beauty of the smaller church and the possibilities that exist in each one. The members of that church taught me to love smaller churches and inspired me to continue working with those churches.

As this book illustrates, Hebron and all small churches will face rapid change in the future unlike any they have ever known. They will be forced to change as well or find themselves incapable of ministering in the twenty-first century. Yet the same God who first called them into existence will continue to be with them during these transitions and will use them to minister to others in ways they cannot now comprehend. My years at Hebron taught me that smaller churches can change, and because of that I want to dedicate this book to the wonderful people I served at Hebron Baptist Church.

CONTENTS

ACKNOWLEDGMENTS

This is the third book I have written with Beacon Hill Press of Kansas City, and once again they have made this an incredible project. Richard Buckner has again been my editor, and his insights and editing have greatly improved my original work. He stretches my thinking and forces me to write with greater clarity. Perhaps more important is the encouragement he gives me throughout the process. Putting ideas on paper is not as easy as some people might believe, and if it wasn't for people who believe in what you do and in the material you write, it would be easy to give up about halfway through. Everyone at Beacon Hill Press of Kansas City has encouraged me throughout every project and has truly been a joy to work with.

Another person who should be recognized is Larry Mason, the executive minister of the American Baptist Churches of Indiana and Kentucky and my boss. Because he sees the importance of smaller churches, he continues to encourage me to write, lead workshops, and develop resources for these churches and their leaders. Without his support I certainly could not serve these churches the way I do.

The person who makes the biggest sacrifice when I write is my wife, Faye. She is the one left alone while I sit at my computer and try to put my thoughts on paper. For 42 years she has been my greatest supporter and my best friend. I thank God for her every day.

To my friends at Beacon Hill, to Larry, and to Faye, I can only say thank you to each of you for making this book possible.

INTRODUCTION

Any book that uses "small church" and "transformation" in the same sentence can't be serious. Transforming a small church certainly sounds like an oxymoron. Everybody knows that small churches resist every effort to change them. We've all known or heard stories of pastors who tried to introduce change to a small church and were soon introduced to the door and, perhaps, to another profession.

Although many small churches are very resistant to change, others are open to change if it is done correctly. Some of these churches look at their decreasing numbers, the increased average age of their people, and the little real ministry that occurs in their congregations, and they know if they don't change some things, their churches won't be around much longer.

Other churches have not declined but have plateaued in attendance. These relatively healthy churches may be small, but they still are active, vital churches that provide good ministry to their members and their surrounding communities. But as they look at their communities, they see great changes taking place. People are looking for different things from a church than they used to. New cultures are moving into the neighborhood. New languages are heard on the street, new foods are available in the local Wal-Mart, and signs in languages other than English are seen in the stores. Industry jobs have disappeared and have been replaced with service jobs. New homes are being built at a rapid pace, the local streets are full of cars, and the population is growing while church attendance remains stagnant.

As denominational churches study their communities, they notice something else. There are a lot of new, nondenominational churches that have recently opened, and they are attracting more people than many of the old, established churches combined. The music in these churches is different. The people attending these churches dress more casually. These churches often use video projectors and have skits in their worship services. People who attend these new churches talk about how relevant the messages are to their lives.

As the smaller, established churches notice all the changes taking place, they realize that if they are going to continue to provide ministry to their communities, they must change the way they do certain things. They can't depend on people coming to them simply because their doors are open and they have the right denominational labels on their church signs. Transformation can occur in these churches because they are more interested in serving God and their communities than they are in holding on to some outdated form of ministry that is no longer relevant to today's culture.

The dying, plateaued church can also change, but some have been in decline for so long that it is unlikely they will do so. These churches are locked into a survival mode and only hope to survive as long as possible. Throughout the book we will see various reasons why smaller churches resist change, but we might as well admit now that transformation will not occur in some churches that are near the end of their ministries. Perhaps the kindest thing that could be done for these churches is to honor their former ministries and allow them to die their natural deaths.

I also believe that some unhealthy small churches can still experience transformation and regain their former healthy ministries. These churches will have to break out of their maintenance mode and become more missional. They will have to catch a fresh vision from God and have the courage to follow that vision. It will require much hard work, earnest prayer, and intentionality, but life-giving change can occur if a church is willing to do these things. This book is designed to assist the pastors and lay leaders in smaller churches bring such change to their churches.

In the first chapter we will examine in more detail the need for transformation. Chapter 2 will explore some of the rapid changes occurring in society that are driving the need for change in the church, and the remaining chapters will look at the various elements of introducing change to churches.

At this point you may be wondering why I have written a book that addresses change in smaller churches. This is my fifth book, and all five of them have been developed for smaller churches and their leaders. For one thing, I love small churches. For twenty years I served as a pastor of a small, rural church that experienced much change during that time. In my current ministry I work with many small churches that are struggling with some of the issues I address in this book, and I have a passion to see them overcome those issues and provide effective, productive ministry to their communities.

Even more important than my experience with small churches, I write for small churches because I believe they provide a much-needed ministry today. I appreciate the megachurches and the great ministries they provide, but there are many more people currently attending the smaller churches in this country than attend the megachurches. Frankly, I don't see that changing. Despite its limited resources and programming, many people prefer the atmosphere of the smaller church to a large church. They enjoy the community that often exists in the smaller church, and they are willing to sacrifice some of the programming a larger church can offer for that sense of community.

If the reader is serious about wanting to see change occur in the small church, he or she must be willing to take a long-term approach. We'll explore this in more detail in a later chapter, but you should understand now that transformation is not an overnight event in any church, and especially in the smaller church. Unless you are willing to make a long-term commitment to change, you would probably be wise to stop reading right now.

You should also know that it is unlikely the church will experience any significant transformation unless its leaders experience it first in their own lives. The type of transformation we will examine in this book is not merely tweaking the system a little here and there. You and your church will be challenged to rethink what it means to be a church and what ministry should look like in the twenty-first century.

If you are a seminary-trained minister, this book may challenge much of what you learned about ministry. I only ask that as you read, you also listen to the Holy Spirit to hear what He might be saying to you. Be warned—listening to the Spirit of God transformed people in the Bible and continues to do so today. It can be scary to hear the voice of God, especially for persons who do not want to experience change in their lives, but it is in listening to—and obeying—that voice that we experience life. As a leader of your church, that life should be what you want for your church.

A CHANGING WORLD
requires a
changing church

We live in a rapidly changing world that requires the church to examine its entire focus on ministry. This first section will look at some of the changes that the church will need to make and how best to address those changes in a not-so-mega church. Some of these changes will be relatively minor, while others will be much more challenging. One of the things to remember is that your church is going to change. As a leader in your church, you have the opportunity to determine whether or not these changes will be positive.

ONE

Missional vs. Maintenance Churches

> *The Church is by nature missionary to the*
> *extent that, if it ceases to be missionary,*
> *it has not just failed in one of its tasks, it*
> *has ceased being the church.*[1]
>
> —J. Andrew Kirk

Every church began as the result of someone's vision for a ministry that was needed in its community. In the area where I live, the landscape is dotted with little churches that are 175 to 200 years old. I can leave my house right now and drive to at least three dozen churches within fifteen minutes. But when these churches were established, the people walked or rode horses and buggies to the churches, and it was important to have one in every community that was easily accessible to the people. Each of these churches began as a way to minister to the surrounding community. They were truly missional churches.

Today that mission has often been replaced with a maintenance mind-set. As these churches begin to decline in attendance, their first instinct is to circle the wagons to preserve the limited resources they have. They call pastors to lead them, but they are really seeking chaplains who will tend to their needs. These churches express a desire to reach youth and young families, but conflict will often occur if this actually happens.

A small church that had been in decline for many years was seeking a new pastor. They said they wanted a pastor who could grow their youth group because "the youth are the future of the church." A few months after their new pastor began, I met a young woman who served on the search committee. I asked if their pastor had been successful in reaching young people. She said he had been very successful, but there was now another problem. The older members were upset that the pastor was spending too much time with the youth and felt that he was ignoring them. As a result, they had stopped attending church and stopped their financial support. After serving there for only three years, this pastor was asked to resign.

Another church experienced similar conflict when the pastor began reaching young families. Complaints soon surfaced about the pastor's clique. The complainers said he spent all his time with this group of people while ignoring others. An "us versus them" mentality soon began to infect the church. The denominational leader who worked with this church quickly identified the complainers as the long-term power brokers in the church who needed to preserve the church's status quo in order to retain their power and influence.

Such maintenance mentality may be due to power issues, survival instincts, or simply because that is all the church has ever known. However, when a church is more focused on maintenance and survival than it is on mission, it has already ceased being the church. If our smaller churches have any hope of surviving, they will have to once again become more missional in their thinking.

MISSIONAL CHURCHES

Maintenance churches see mission as something they support. They give money to denominational and parachurch agencies that are involved in "mission work" around the world. They may invite missionaries to speak to their church about the exciting work they are doing in some remote location. Such churches see mission as done somewhere else by somebody else. In contrast to this way of thinking is that of the missional church.

Although missional churches often support mission efforts in other locations, they also understand that their mission is found in their own communities. They take seriously Jesus' call to be a witness to their Jerusalem, and they understand that it is the responsibility of every member of the church to be missionaries to that community. Mission isn't something that is done by someone else but is the responsibility of every believer in Jesus Christ, and missional churches spend time and resources equipping people to be missionaries.

> *And you shall be witnesses to me in Jerusalem, and in all Judea and Samaria, and to the end of the earth.*
>
> —Acts 1:8

A NEW PHILOSOPHY

This requires not just a new way of working but a new way of thinking for many churches: "Mission is not something the church does, a part of its total program. No, the church's existence is missional, for the calling and sending action of God forms its identity. Mission is founded on the mission of God in the world, rather than the church's effort to extend itself."[2]

Although church mission ministries can be expressed locally, nationally, and internationally, mission is not first about geography but philosophy. It is not about *where* the church is but *who* the church is and *what it is here to accomplish.* It is not location-based but relation-based. Wherever believers are, those among whom they live and work constitute the mission field. Being missional is not first about ministering among those we do not know but about living authentically among those we do know.[3]

At one time it could be claimed that America was a Christian nation. At the very least, one would have to agree that life in America was shaped around the teachings of Scripture, and the church had a great influence on the morals and practices of the people. Neither of these are now true. We now live in a nation that has embraced many different religions and philosophies. Christianity has been relegated to the periphery of most people's lives, if it is even on their radar screens at all. Our age is often referred to as pre-Christian or postmodern, and some Christian leaders even claim that we are now trying to do ministry in a pagan society.[4] We are fast approaching a time when non-Christians will outnumber Christians in America.

This means that our churches need to see themselves as mission stations working in a non-Christian culture. When a person prepares to become a missionary to a people group, he or she may need to learn new languages, a different culture, different clothing styles, different customs, and even to eat different foods. To be effective the missionary has to fit into the new culture. It is not the job of the missionary to Americanize the culture being served but to introduce Jesus Christ to the people in that culture.

This is the challenge of the church that truly wants to be effective in reaching this generation God has given us. We can no longer sit back in our pews, invite people to come to our services, and ask them to adapt to our culture so we can tell them about Jesus. We have to understand their culture and learn their language and new ways of doing ministry so we can share the good news of Jesus Christ with them in ways they can understand. This is a completely different philosophy of how to "do church" than many of our smaller churches currently have. Smaller churches that seek to become missional will have to change several things about the way they now do things.

MISSIONAL CHURCHES ARE FOCUSED

Although the missionaries I have known are very talented people who are able to do many different things, their primary ministry is rather focused. They tend to work for long periods of time with the same people groups often within a limited geographical area. Early in life they understood God's calling on their lives, and they spend the rest of their lives fulfilling that calling.

Small, maintenance-minded churches prefer to take a broad view of ministry. I have frequently encouraged struggling smaller churches to identify a target group they could try to serve and focus their efforts on that group. In nearly every case, my efforts have been rejected. Leaders of these churches always respond with the same argument: God has called us to reach out to everyone. They take a shotgun approach to ministry, hoping something they do touches the life of somebody rather than focusing on a specific target and concentrating their efforts on reaching that target group. They usually end up touching no one.

Saddleback Church has identified a target they refer to as Saddleback Sam. They have created a very detailed composite of Saddleback Sam, and everyone who goes through their membership classes can clearly describe the characteristics of Saddleback Sam. In fact, they can clearly identify him because he is their next-door neighbor.[5]

Willow Creek Church identified their target audience and named that audience Unchurched Harry and Unchurched Mary. This church has also clearly identified the characteristics of this couple, and they focus their ministry efforts on reaching their target.[6]

Each of these churches has many thousands of people attend their worship services each week. Their financial and human resources far exceed those of smaller churches, and yet they understand that no church has the resources to reach out to every person in its community. They have identified the target group they believe God has asked them to reach, and they focus their efforts to reach that group. This decision then impacts the music they use in their worship services, how the church facilities are laid out and decorated, how the messages are presented, how literature is prepared, and even how people are greeted when they arrive on the property.

Compare this to the smaller church with a hundred people (or less) in the worship service on a typical Sunday morning. Their music is also targeted toward people (their existing members), their sermons are delivered in a way that is appealing to their targeted audience (their existing members), people are welcomed to the church in a way that is appealing to their targeted audience (their existing members), as is everything else they do. The only targeted group most smaller churches seek to serve is their existing members, and they wonder why they can't reach new people.

> *God's mission is calling and sending us, the church of Jesus Christ, to be a missionary church in our own societies, in the cultures in which we find ourselves.*[7]
>
> —Darrell L. Guder

If a church is serious about wanting to be missional, it must identify a target different from its existing members. A missional church will seek God's direction to identify a people group within their community and begin to focus its efforts and ministry toward reaching those people. The more narrow the focus, the more effective the church is apt to be in reaching them. Such a church is truly on mission with God.

MISSIONAL CHURCHES HAVE HIGH EXPECTATIONS FOR THEIR MEMBERS

Maintenance churches are very concerned about their members and will do just about anything to ensure that no one leave the church. Harmony is often preferred over truth or mission.[8] Church membership guarantees certain perks: free weddings for your children, free funerals, and the right to select the music and the times of the worship services. Stewardship is ignored because the membership doesn't like to hear sermons about money. There is little emphasis on discipleship, and as a result, few adults are found in Sunday School classes or small groups. Maintenance churches do not ask their members to be involved in any meaningful ministry outside the church, and even if they did, the members are kept so busy serving on committees designed to preserve the organization that they wouldn't have time for ministry. If members drop out of active involvement in the life of the church, their names are simply moved over to the "inactive member" list.

Missional churches don't have "inactive member" lists. These churches have high expectations for their members, and they are not afraid to communicate those expectations to people before they become members.[9] Many of these churches require persons seeking membership in the church to complete a membership class in which these expectations are clearly explained. Some require a signed membership covenant agreement that states that the new member will fulfill their expectations of membership.

Two other things occur in missional churches that don't happen in maintenance churches. Extensive training is provided the membership so they can better understand their spiritual gifts and how they can use those gifts in ministering to others. Second, the administrative work done by committees is turned over to the pastoral staff, and the church structure is streamlined so people have the time and energy to be involved in ministry.

TRAIN THE SAINTS

Late in my pastorate I became convicted that, like many pastors, I was better at complaining that few of our members were involved in any type of ministry than I was in helping prepare them for ministry. I also became aware that there are many in our congregations who want to be more involved in ministry but are waiting for someone to train them. That someone, according to Eph. 4:11-12, is the pastor: "And He Himself gave some to be apostles, some prophets, some evangelists, and some pastors and teachers, for the equipping of the saints for the work of ministry, for the edifying of the body of Christ."

It is not the responsibility of the pastor to do the entire ministry that occurs in the church but to equip the members to do that ministry. Maintenance churches believe otherwise. This might be a slight exaggeration, but there are some church members who want to call the pastor every time their cat stubs its toe, and they expect the pastor to hurry right over to conduct a healing service for the cat! These same members later complain about the lack of growth in the church and usually assign the blame to that same pastor.

Rather than focusing on pastoral care, missional churches understand that congregational care is the more biblical model.[10] If the pastor is expected to provide all the caring ministry in the church, it should not be surprising that the church is unable to grow. There are only so many people one person can care for. However, if the congregation accepts responsibility for caring for one another, there is no limit to the growth potential of the church.

> *We expect both too much and the wrong kinds of things from pastors, much of which should be done by other church members.*[11]
> —Klyne Snodgrass

Congregational care cannot occur if the pastor does not provide the training and resources church members need in order to feel comfortable in a ministry role. Laypeople are often reluctant to visit someone in the hospital, nursing home, or funeral home because they don't know what they will say when they get there. They fear accepting leadership positions because they are afraid they will fail and the church will suffer. They avoid opportunities to share their faith with others because they aren't sure how to do so, and they are afraid someone will ask questions they are not equipped to answer. Fear is the number one reason laypeople are not more involved in ministry, and this fear can only be eliminated when they are properly trained in how to do these things.

Pastors must take the time to identify potential servant leaders in the church and invest themselves in the lives of these individuals. It is crucial for the future of the church that the pastoral leaders help these persons feel comfortable doing ministry. Such comfort will only happen when they have been challenged to do ministry and given the tools to do it well.

SIMPLIFY THE STRUCTURE

If we want our church members involved in ministry, we must also take away much of the administrative work they are now asked to do. Please understand, there is nothing evil about administration. Organizations, including churches, must be properly managed in order to effectively operate. The problem is that most administration is maintenance work, and too often we so overwhelm our church members with maintenance work that they have no time or energy to do ministry.

I consulted in one small church that complained that the few people who were willing to be involved were often sitting on six or seven committees in addition to serving as teachers, choir members, and other roles in the church. Several admitted that many of these committees never met because people just didn't have the energy and time to attend everything they were asked to attend. The church was not growing; it had financial problems; there was a great deal of conflict; and many people were blaming the pastor for these problems.

Despite very nice facilities in an excellent location, this church had a structure that inhibited growth. Most of the church's energy was focused internally in their committee (maintenance) responsibilities. Few people felt any great desire to minister in the community, and their many responsibilities within the church would have prevented such ministry anyway. I asked why each of these committees existed, and the only reason given for many of them was that they were required by the church's constitution! Part of my recommendation to the church was to eliminate the committees that added little to the life of the church, and that recommendation was promptly rejected.

I'm convinced that the majority of committees in most small churches could stop meeting, and the congregation would see no impact on the life of the church. Many smaller churches are over-structured for their size. They have so many boards and committees that they have to ask their few members to sit on several of them in order to fill all the slots, and many of these boards and committees really don't add much to the life of the church. They add even less to the

> *The church of the twenty-first century must shift its focus from an institutional orientation to a community orientation.*[12]
> —Mike Regele

mission effectiveness of the church. People either have time to serve on committees or be involved in ministry. Only if a committee exists to serve a true ministry need within the church or community is serving on that committee a good use of people's time.

You may be wondering who would be responsible for seeing that administrative work is done in the church. In the missional church that task is done by the pastor and a few key leaders who are especially gifted and called to this role. Decisions are entrusted to these leaders who are expected to make their decisions based on the core values and vision of the church.[13]

This will be a very difficult paradigm shift for many smaller churches, and, quite frankly, an impossible change for others. In the Baptist tradition of which I am a member we have as one of our chief tenets the belief that the congregation makes the decisions that impact the church. Committees, boards, and individuals make proposals at the regularly scheduled or special-called business meetings, and the people attending the meeting listen to the proposals and vote whether or not to approve them. We seem to believe that the will of God is determined by a 51 percent majority vote. (The decision of the Israelites to not enter the Promised Land the first time should be sufficient to disprove this theory! [Num. 13—14].)

Despite the biblical example, this will still be a difficult change for congregational churches to make and will require a great deal of trust within the church. Many factors impact the level of trust that exists within a church, and a low level of trust will ensure that the congregation will insist on voting on virtually every proposal made within the church. If little trust exists in the church, it would probably be best to work on this issue first before trying to make the shift away to the leaders assuming full responsibility for the administrative functions of the church.

However, there are two good reasons for making the move away from having the congregation vote on every proposal that comes before the church. One, change is happening so fast that congregational decision making is always playing catch-up. By the time a committee or board discusses a proposal for a few months and the church finally has a chance to vote on it, many of the benefits of the proposal may already have been lost. New ministries and opportunities may be presenting themselves, but the church is still discussing the original proposals, causing them to miss these new opportunities as well. Congregational decision making was fine in a slower age, but in the twenty-first century it is vital that decisions be made quickly so the changes can be implemented in time to have the most effective impact.

A second reason to entrust decision making in the hands of a few is that these are the people who have studied an issue and developed a proposal that addresses it. If a ministry team has spent several weeks, or even months, researching a significant change for the church, how can we expect a few people who attend a business meeting to intelligently vote on the proposal after hearing it discussed for a few minutes? They can't, and many churches have lost the opportunity to provide more effective ministries to their communities because people did not understand a proposed change and voted against it.

Clearly there are dangers involved in handing over decision-making power to a few people within the church. Some might make decisions based on selfish or unbiblical reasons. If that happens, the church must have a mechanism in place to remove such people from the decision-making body. Decisions might be based upon faulty information, but that can also happen in a congregational decision-making process. While there are risks associated with entrusting decision-making power to a few, there are also risks in not doing so. This leads us to our next characteristic of missional churches.

MISSIONAL CHURCHES TAKE RISKS

Maintenance churches are committed to self-preservation and will do little that might threaten their continued existence. Missional churches understand that being on mission automatically assumes there is risk involved, and such risk does not frighten them. In fact, missional leaders are just as concerned about the risk involved in not taking some action as they are in the risk associated with going forward.[15]

Risk must be evaluated not by the fear it generates in you or the probability of success, but by the value of the goal.[14]

—John Maxwell

Two years ago I was asked to speak to a small church that was in serious decline and present a process to help them identify a fresh vision from God for their church. In my presentation I mentioned that there is always the possibility that if the church begins to implement some changes, some people might leave the church. Those changes do not reflect who they are or what they want from a church, and they will feel it is necessary to leave. I emphasized that I was not saying that people would leave the church but that they might. Following the service the church had a question-and-answer session that was going well until one elderly lady reminded the church of my comment that people might leave. She said, "When you said that, I looked around the sanctuary and didn't see anyone I was willing to lose." Several heads nodded in agreement, and I never heard from that church again. The risk of losing a friend in the church was too great. In my opinion, that church has a much greater risk of seeing their doors close within the next decade, but that is a risk they are willing to take.

Risk is a normal part of progress and growth. The founding fathers risked everything when they declared independence from England. The risks were huge when early settlers began moving west in hopes of finding a new life. Your church exists today because at one time people took the risk of starting a new church to provide Christian teaching and ministry to the community. Many older churches have risked moving their meeting sites to new locations in the belief this would allow them to offer better ministry. In each of these situations the people involved understood the risks but believed the benefits of moving forward with their plans were greater than the risks. Our smaller churches will have to adopt the same belief if they want to successfully move from being maintenance-minded to missional.

Courage is not the absence of fear. Courage assumes fear.[16]
—Andy Stanley

A question I often ask churches who are struggling with the risks associated with transformation is, "Who are we here for?" If our churches and their ministries exist solely for the benefit of the membership, then we really don't need to make any changes and risk upsetting people and disrupting our current ministries. However, if our purpose includes reaching new people for the kingdom of God, then we must be willing to take the risks that will enable us to do that.

The purpose of every church is to fulfill the Great Commission and the Great Commandment. Both involve risk. It is risky to share our faith in the pluralistic, post-modern world in which we live today. It is risky to love people unconditionally. But it is riskier to disobey God's will, and the benefits of being obedient to God's purpose for our churches are far greater than the risks.

> *The church is one of the few organizations in the world that does not exist for the benefit of its members.*[17]
> —Ed Stetzer and David Putman

Only when we are willing to accept the risks and share our faith and love people as God does will we see lives transformed by the grace and power of God.

WHY ARE MISSIONAL CHURCHES SO IMPORTANT?

One can travel to many churches that are struggling to survive today and find somewhere on their walls a picture taken in the early to mid-twentieth century that shows a congregation that filled the church every Sunday. One church told me that in the mid-1900s not only was their sanctuary full every Sunday, but in the summer they would open the windows and people would sit outside on the grass or in their vehicles to hear the preacher. That church today will normally have three to four dozen people attend their morning worship service. The denominational affiliation of this church has not changed, nor has its location. The facility is much more modern today—with air-conditioning, carpeting, padded pews, a beautiful new fellowship area with a modern kitchen, and a paved parking area. They remain theologically conservative. The difference is not in the church; it is in the society in which they are trying to do ministry.

We live in a time of rapid change such as has never been seen before. While the maintenance church seeks to maintain its traditions and offers ministries in ways that used to be successful, the world around them is changing at a mind-boggling rate. Some of those changes are the subject of the next chapter, but we can say here that we need missional churches because they are the only churches that will not see these changes as a threat but merely as the new context in which they will minister to their communities.

TWO

Our Changing World

In times of change, learners inherit the earth, while the learned find themselves beautifully equipped to deal with a world which no longer exists.[1]

—Eric Hoffer

As I grew up in the 1950s and 1960s, all the Baptist churches in our county were identical to each other. As we moved around the county, we would join a new church in the new community, but it was hard to tell any real difference between our new church and the one we left. Services started at the same time, the hymnals were the same, the Sunday School literature all came from the denominational publishing house, and the ministries they offered were nearly identical.

Not only were the churches similar to one another, but most people preferred them to be. We were like-minded people practicing a like-minded faith in like-minded ways. When we moved to a new community we looked for a church from our denomination. We didn't want any surprises in our faith, and we were unlikely to experience any.

That is not the case today. We live in a time that celebrates differences. When people move today, they no longer limit their search for a church to one from the same denomination in which they were raised. People look for churches that provide the worship experiences, the ministries and programs, and the style that speaks to them. We are no longer like-minded. In fact, our physical and spiritual needs differ greatly, and our search for a church reflects those differences. Offering the same ministries that we offered thirty and forty years ago will often not meet many of these needs.

Not only are people's needs different, but also our culture is changing rapidly, and many churches are not adapting to those changes very well. One common reason given by people who do not attend church is that they do not find today's church relevant. We provide answers to questions that people no longer ask. Many churches today are still trying to offer flannelgraph ministries to a society that uses computers, Xboxes, cell phones, and iPods. The fact that the spell-checker on my computer doesn't even recognize the word *flannelgraph* speaks volumes about our problem.[2]

MAJOR CHANGES ARE OCCURRING QUICKLY

The changes being experienced in our culture are not minor, and neither are the ones confronting today's church. Loren Mead discusses the differences between transitional and transformational changes. He writes, "Transitional change [means] the adaptations and shifts brought on by temporary dislocations and discomforts, moving to a new stability. . . . Transformational change [is the] shattering of the foundations and the reconstitution of a new entity."[3] Transformational change is the type of change occurring in today's world, and if the church wants to speak to today's culture, it must be willing to experience the same type of change.

The changes are happening rapidly. Let's look at just a few examples:

- A new high-tech product hits the United States marketplace every seventeen seconds,[4] and Americans are buying them. According to *Wired Magazine,* a third of households in this country spend more than $200 a month for these gadgets they believe are essential to their quality of life.[5]

- It took 1,500 years from the year A.D. 1 for knowledge to double. It doubled again in only 250 years, and by 1900 knowledge doubled again. Today knowledge doubles every two years.[6] Some calculate that by 2010 knowledge will double every eleven hours.[7] One futurist predicts, "As much as 97 percent of world knowledge will be accumulated over one person's lifetime."[8]

- For thirty years I worked in a factory. Our union contract provided for early retirement after working thirty years, and in 1996 I was able to retire from that job at forty-seven years of age. Will such benefits be available to the worker of the future? Probably not, since it is predicted that the average person should anticipate eleven job changes during his or her working life. Regardless of your profession, you should plan on reinventing yourself at least every seven years.[9] Persons entering the workforce today should plan on being lifelong learners if they want to remain employable.

- Much of that learning will take place online. Internet use now doubles every 100 days.[10] At the end of 2005 nearly 70 percent of people in North America were online.[11] Some of these persons are getting their degrees. Some are looking up recipes. Others are searching for churches in their communities to attend and seeking spiritual instruction. A quality Web site is considered crucial for churches wanting to reach persons under thirty years of age.[12] Larger churches recognize this, and 91 percent of churches with more than 250 adults attending their services now have Web sites compared to only 48 percent of those churches with less than 100 adults.[13]

- The Hispanic population is now the largest minority in the United States, and the numbers keep growing. The United States Census Bureau estimates that the Hispanic population in the United States will be over 102 million persons by 2050, which will represent slightly over 24 percent of the total population.[14] This will have a huge impact on every church and denomination serious about reaching a quarter of the nation's population for Jesus Christ.

- If you pull into the drive-through lane at a McDonald's restaurant near Cape Girardeau, Missouri, owned by Shannon David, you will not place your order with an employee inside the restaurant. The person taking your order is actually working in a call center in Colorado Springs, Colorado, more than 900 miles away. By the time you arrive at the pick-up window, your photo and order is shown on the screen and your order is waiting for you. The process has worked so well that McDonald's franchise owners in Minnesota and Massachusetts are now using that call center to receive their orders.[15]

Talk about transformational change! Today's high school dropouts can't even be sure they can get a job at McDonald's. We could fill a book with examples of the rapid changes occurring in our world today, but these should be enough to convince the reader that the world we are trying to reach is experiencing incredible changes. These changes alone are enough of a challenge to most small churches, but there are other problems as well. The way people look at the church and their views on biblical teaching are also changing.

PEOPLE WANT DIFFERENT THINGS FROM THE CHURCH

Denominational labels continue to be less important to younger people. Our family may have moved several times when I was growing up, but we always joined a church of the same denomination in our new community. That is less likely to happen today. I continue to serve in that same denomination, but our two children and their families attend nondenominational churches where they live. The denomination in which I minister has been declining for years, but the churches our children attend are growing rapidly and attracting the younger families many denominational churches struggle to reach.

Younger people today are often reluctant to join anything. This has become a problem, not only for the church but also for many organizations such as veterans' groups, service clubs, and other affinity groups. People are willing to be involved in activities to which they are attracted, but they are less likely to join an organization. According to many church constitutions, this automatically excludes them from serving in any official capacity in the church, which in turn deprives the church of their gifts and insights. It also means they are not likely to continue attending a church if they cannot be involved in meaningful ministry. Incidentally, the two churches my children attend do not have membership. If you attend there, you are expected to be involved in the ministry of the church.

A pastor can no longer expect his or her words to carry authority simply because they are biblical. According to George Barna, only one-fourth of adults and just one out of ten teenagers in America believe absolute moral truth exists.[16] If the reader wonders why there is so much chaos in today's society, Barna goes on to explain:

> If there is no absolute truth, then the Bible is not the source of moral truth; and God is, therefore, not the ultimate authority. Without an ultimate authority, there are no universally accepted standards and no reliable principles that lead to righteousness. In fact, without absolute morality, there is no standard of righteousness.[17]

This does not mean that people are not seeking the truth. Some churches today have watered down their message, believing this would make their churches more attractive to the unchurched. In fact, people who are seeking to have their spiritual needs met want a church that is clear about its doctrinal beliefs.[18] Many young adults are questioning the relativism they have been taught, and believe that absolute truth can be known. This is leading many of them to return to traditional religious teachings and morality.[19]

This is good news, but it also carries new responsibilities. People today want to know how these truths impact their lives. They ask questions different from the past. I've never had anyone approach me wanting to know how to be justified, and few people have asked how they could have their sins forgiven. However, I've had several people want to talk about the chaos and pain in their lives and wonder if God has anything to say about that. People want to know their lives have meaning and purpose, and relativism cannot offer that to anyone. God can, and many people want to hear how they can experience that in their lives.

Churches that find culturally appropriate ways to meet people's felt needs for ultimate meaning will succeed, and those that do not will fail.[20]
—Donald E. Miller

One thing we must avoid with today's culture is stating doctrinal truth with the assumption that our listeners will understand what we are saying. The fact is that many, including those inside the church, are biblically illiterate. There was a time when even unbelievers understood the basic teachings of Christianity, but that day is far past.

In the mid-1990s I was talking to a young mother about her relationship with God. She informed me that she had never been inside a church in her life and didn't know enough about God to even ask a good question. We began to talk about her need for Jesus Christ in her life, and every few minutes she would stop me. I was speaking "Churchese," and she didn't understand the language. I had to interpret my words so she could understand. It took several months, but she finally invited Jesus Christ into her life and became one of the most active members in our church. Today, we should always assume that people, including some within our congregations, will not understand biblical teaching, and we must take the time to clarify even the most basic doctrines of the Christian faith.

Teaching biblical truth must involve both the mind and the heart. Jesus engaged people with both truth and compassion. As He moved about the countryside, He encountered suffering people. He didn't ignore their felt needs as He taught them truth. He ministered to the blind, the lame, the leprous, and those trapped in deep sins while He spoke with great authority. Our churches must follow His example. People in our postmodern culture want to see our faith in action, and they will be much more responsive to the message we proclaim when they see it lived out in our lives for the good of all.

Worship must also engage the mind and heart. "Postmoderns literally 'feel' their way through life."[21] Many of them will not be attracted to a worship experience in which people merely go through the motions of following a printed program. They need to feel that they are connecting with God through the worship. Such worship will require more interaction between the worship leaders and the congregation than we normally see in smaller churches. It will also include more visual stimulation than many of our churches provide.

The greatest apologetic for the gospel is and always has been a community that actually lives by the gospel.[22]

—Brian D. McLaren

The senior saints who make up most of the membership in many smaller churches grew up listening to the radio. Today, most people prefer watching television than merely listening to a radio. We don't even just listen to music anymore; we watch the videos that have been created for the songs. We are a visually stimulated society, and many of us prefer the visual to the spoken.

This was recently driven home to me in a new way. In an interview Jay Leno was asked about the changes to the *Tonight Show* since he became the host. Leno replied that one of the changes was the addition of visual gags in the monologue. He noticed many people were telling him that they had heard his monologue and were complimenting him on it. He thought about that for a while and realized something was wrong. Television is a visual medium, but people were talking about listening to the monologue. He decided then to have video clips inserted in different places during the monologue.

I hesitate to even mention the music in our worship services because of how it has divided so many churches. We must come to terms with the understanding that there is no one correct style of church music, and different styles are going to appeal to different groups within the worship service. Your church has the right to select the type of music it will allow in the worship services, but be aware that the music you select will have a tremendous impact on the future of your church.

The style of music you choose to use in your services will be one of the most critical (and controversial) decisions you make in the life of your church. It may also be the most influential factor in determining who your church reaches for Christ and whether or not your church grows. . . . Once you have decided on the style of music you're going to use in worship, you have set the direction of your church in far more ways than you realize. It will determine the kind of people you attract, the kind of people you keep, and the kind of people you lose.[23]

It is not uncommon for a church today to have four or even five generations attending the services. The music tastes of each generation differ greatly. Think about the music your grandparents listened to and compare that to the music you preferred growing up. Did you and your parents ever have any arguments over your music? Why should we be surprised when those arguments occur in church between different generations?

> *There is no such thing as "Christian music." There are only "Christian lyrics."*[24]
>
> —Rick Warren

There are only two criteria for good worship music: it must be biblical, and it must enable a person to experience God. The style of music isn't relevant. I encourage you to go to your local music store and see how many people buy organ music. I doubt that anyone enjoys only one style of music outside of the church, so why do we think we can only have one style inside the church?

I am not too many years from retirement age, and I enjoy the great hymns of the faith. I also enjoy southern gospel music. In fact, my wife and I are permanent seat holders at the National Quartet Convention held each year in Louisville, Kentucky. We usually attend all six nights, and on the first night I purchase my tickets for the upcoming year.

I also enjoy the Blind Boys of Alabama with their more bluesy renditions of gospel music. We attended one of their performances earlier this year, and it was a very enjoyable and worshipful evening. There are many styles of music I enjoy, and as long as they meet the criteria mentioned above, they are all suitable for worship.

One style of music I do not particularly care for is praise music. Some people call them 7-11 songs (seven words sung eleven times)! But I can sing them and worship with them because I know that others around me are connecting with God as we worship through that style of music. It's not about me and my preferences; it's about allowing people to experience God.

As I work with small churches, they continually lament their lack of younger families and youth. When I visit their worship services, it soon becomes apparent why they struggle to reach those groups. Their worship services are geared toward those who have been attending the church all their lives. The pace is slow, the music uninspiring, the sermon delivered in a droning monotone, and at the end of the service everyone hurriedly leaves, greatly inspired to eat lunch. That is not what people today seek in a worship experience.

Somewhere I read a story about the pastor of a small church who felt the need to add more contemporary music in the worship services that would appeal to a younger age-group. He hesitantly brought the subject up in the church business meeting and waited for the reaction from the church patriarch. The pastor correctly understood that the patriarch's attitude toward this change would determine how the rest of the church would respond.

After the pastor finished speaking, there was a time of silence while everyone's eyes were on the patriarch. Slowly, he began to pull himself up from his pew and spoke, "I don't like the kind of music our pastor is recommending we use in our services. I don't like to hear it; I don't like to be around it." He paused for a few seconds and continued speaking, "But if we don't do something my grandson is going to die and go to hell! I'm in favor of doing this in an effort to reach him and others of his age." He slowly began to sit back down.

The pastor breathed a quiet sigh of relief, and the others attending the meeting smiled in agreement of what was just said. Then the old patriarch began to rise again. He said, "But I'm not going to sing those songs!"[25]

And that was all right. He rightly understood it wasn't about him; it was for those the church had not yet reached with the gospel. Remember the question, Who are we here for? If we are just here for ourselves, it really isn't important if we understand the culture in which we do ministry. If we enjoy the status quo, we can leave things alone, worship God as we always have, and look forward to the day when He calls us all home. But if we are here to take the kingdom of God to those who have not yet received Jesus as Lord and Savior, then we must be willing to reach out to others on their terms.

> *The North American church is suffering from severe amnesia. It has forgotten why it exists.*[26]
> —Reggie McNeal

Even when we answer the question correctly, it doesn't mean that change will be easy. Introducing change in any organization is difficult, and it is especially so in a small church. However, getting the right answer to the question does give us a foundation upon which to base these changes. In the remaining chapters of this book we will explore how to introduce and implement the needed changes that will enable your church to significantly impact the lives of those people God has given you to serve. But before we do that, we must look at the importance of leadership in the successful transformation of a church to a missional mind-set.

THREE

Transformational Leadership

*The key to the formation of missional
communities is their leadership.*[1]
—Alan J. Roxburgh

The histories of the divided kingdoms of Israel and Judah are interesting studies in leadership. Both kingdoms had nineteen kings during this period. The Bible refers to each of Israel's kings as evil because they led the people away from worshipping God and into idolatry. As a result, the kingdom of Israel only lasted a little over 200 years before being carried away into Assyrian captivity.

Some of Judah's kings were also evil and led their people into idolatry, but other kings brought religious reform to the land. They tore down the false places of worship and restored the worship of Yahweh and a respect for His Word. During the reign of the godly kings, God blessed and protected the land, and as a result, Judah survived about 345 years before being conquered by the Babylonians.

What is similar in both situations is that the people followed the example of their leaders. The people were willing to worship false deities when being governed by ungodly kings, but they quickly reverted back to worshipping Yahweh when being led by the godly leaders. If small churches experience transformation, it will only occur if their leaders are first experiencing transformation in their own lives and are committed to moving the church from being maintenance-minded to mission-minded. This chapter will explore some of the traits that the leadership must have if our smaller churches will successfully experience such transformation.

WHAT TYPE OF LEADERSHIP IS NEEDED?

There are many ways to understand leadership. Some view leadership in terms of power and authority, and such an understanding of leadership would include everyone from the president of the United States to the head of a crime family. Others would define leadership as influence, and this description would include people such as Mother Teresa, who had a tremendous influence on people through her example of loving and caring for those most helpless and alone. However, that definition would also include a person such as Britney Spears, who influences the clothing styles and music tastes of millions of young people. While both ways of understanding leadership can be valid, and both are needed for church transformation to occur, neither of these go far enough to describe the type of leadership that is needed to make the transformational changes required by our churches. Adaptive leadership is needed for the church to be able to respond to the rapid changes occurring around us.

Adaptive leadership is not leadership with all the answers. It is leadership that is willing to experiment with ideas, keeping those that work and quickly eliminating those that do not. Such leaders are willing to continually learn new ways of doing ministry that will enable the church to achieve its God-given purposes. This type of leadership helps the church understand the gap that exists between its current thinking and practices and the changing environment in which it does ministry. Leadership of this kind also assists the church in making the adjustments and changes necessary to enjoy a successful ministry in the new environment.[2]

Frankly, not every leader is able to do this. Most of us are more comfortable with making minor changes rather than larger ones. For good reason, many small church leaders are fearful of suggesting large-scale changes because they know such suggestions will not be well received by those who want to maintain the current situation. Others are simply afraid of failing.

The fear of failing has paralyzed more than one church leader—both clergy and lay. We know how to do what we've always done. It may not lead us to what we would like to experience, but it is comfortable, and we know we can do it. Responding to the changes in our environment takes us out of our comfort zone. It calls us to do new things, and

> *To achieve your dreams, you must embrace adversity and make failure a regular part of your life. If you're not failing, you're probably not really moving forward.*[3]
>
> —John Maxwell

we don't know if we can do them. For many of us, we've not been taught how to do ministry like that. Seminaries teach ministerial students how to do research and manage; most do not teach their students adaptive leadership skills, but it is the adaptive skills that will enable us to bring transformation to our churches.

LEADERS NEED TRAINING IN MISSIONAL MINISTRY

One reason so many smaller churches operate in a maintenance mind-set is that their leaders have been trained as managers. Seminaries train their students in skills such as counseling, preaching, church administration, and pastoral care. These skills are important, but they were designed for a church that no longer exists.[4] If seminaries want to provide the education required for missional leaders, they must develop a new curriculum that will address the issues facing churches and these leaders today.

When I've previously written about seminary education, I have been criticized by some as being anti-education. That is not true. In fact, a month before writing this section of the book I completed a master of arts in religion from a well-respected seminary, and I am now enrolled in a doctor of ministry program from that same seminary. I believe bivocational and small church ministers must continually find ways to learn new skills and acquire additional knowledge in order to be more effective ministers.

The criticism I sometimes offer is directed at educational programs that neither prepare people for ministry in the real world that exists in the twenty-first century nor equip those who will be serving in smaller churches. I am not alone in that criticism. Aubrey Malphurs, a professor at Dallas Theological Seminary and respected author, shares the same concerns:

A scan of the typical seminary curriculum would reveal that far too many are not aware of what is taking place in North American culture and its impact on the typical church. Though many seminaries and Christian colleges have begun to use the new technology, they are typically business as usual when it comes to the curriculum.

My view is that the problem is not what evangelical seminaries teach but what they do not teach. Many evangelical seminaries teach the Bible and theology, and it is imperative that they do so. However, they often do not provide strong training in leadership, people skills, and strategic-thinking skills and this is poor preparation for ministry in today's shrinking world, which is undergoing intense, convoluted change.[5]

Leith Anderson notes that "traditional seminary education is designed to train research theologians, who are to become parish practitioners. Probably they are adequately equipped for neither."[6]

Anthony Pappas, executive minister of the American Baptist Churches of Massachusetts, served as a bivocational pastor of a small church for several years and has written a number of excellent books on small church ministry. He writes:

> Given the state of the local church today, pastors need to be able to introduce substantial change, build social, cultural and programmatic structures that did not exist when they arrived, and constantly adapt to changing environmental dynamics. In short the role we should be preparing pastors for is that of entrepreneur![7]

I agree with Malphurs that our churches need the theological training students receive from seminaries and Bible schools. It is essential that our churches be led by individuals who are well grounded theologically and who hold to a sound Christian worldview. But we also need the entrepreneurial leader who can provide vision and lead the church in accomplishing God's vision for the church. Many seminaries now offer various master of arts in religion degrees in addition to their standard master of divinity degree to better equip ministers in the more practical aspects of pastoral ministry. The seminary from which I earned my degree offered several tracks in its master of arts in religion program. I took the one with a concentration in leadership. It offered a good mix of theological training and practical ministry skills that should be very beneficial to the person called to serve in smaller churches.

A necessary skill for the entrepreneurial, missional leader is the ability to understand the context in which the church does ministry. We are living in times of great change. It is the responsibility of the leader to interpret those changes to the congregation and lead them in discovering a ministry that will be effective in the context in which they serve.

I began my pastoral ministry at Hebron Baptist Church in 1981. When I resigned as pastor in 2001 to become an area minister, the way I went about ministry had changed in many ways. Some of these changes occurred because I learned new methods of doing ministry; some of them changed because people's expectations and needs had changed; and some of them changed because the old methods were simply not effective anymore. Ministers and churches who insist on providing the same ministries regardless of how ineffective those ministries may become are not missional but preoccupied with maintaining traditions and rituals. Missional leaders must be able to see the changes occurring in society and how the church can best respond to those changes and then begin to lead the church in that response.

One is too small a number to achieve greatness.[8]
—John C. Maxwell

Another quality of missional leaders is that they understand they are most effective when working as part of a team. Solo ministers simply cannot provide effective ministry in this postmodern era. The needs are too diverse, and the opportunities are too great. Regardless of the size of the church, ministry teams will enable more effective ministry to occur.

Many people think of paid staff when they think of a ministry team, so they automatically assume smaller churches that may not even be able to afford a fully funded pastor surely could not have a ministry team. Nothing could be farther from the truth. If I were to return to pastoral ministry in a small church, I would start by identifying people in the church who could form a team not only to help me better understand their church but also to begin visualizing and developing new ministries to help us better serve our community.

If many traditional seminary programs do not train ministers to be entrepreneurial, missional leaders, where can such training be found? Some larger missional churches have developed their own schools of ministry for persons identified within their churches as potential leaders. In some cases, these churches make their programs available to other churches in their community.

Some denominational districts or regions have created ministry training centers for leaders and potential leaders. The region in which I serve developed the Church Leadership Institute, which offers two tracks of study. The first track is a two-year program designed for persons wanting to learn more about the Bible and wanting to be more effective leaders in their churches. A second track adds an additional year of study and was developed for persons who are currently serving in a bivocational ministry position or who sense they might be called to such a position.

There are programs offered through the Internet and on CD-ROM that are designed to fit into the schedule of a busy minister who wants training in practical areas of church leadership. For example, the Moench Center for Church Leadership offers an excellent program on CD-ROM that leads to a Church Leadership Certification. Their studies cover a number of practical ministry skills, called SkillTracks, which would be very helpful to leaders of small churches.[9]

The transformation period is a very difficult time for many churches. It is "an in-between time, when current habits and practices are increasingly dysfunctional yet the future is not discernable."[10] Church members may realize their current practices are no longer effective, but there is still fear in leaving the known for the unknown. Such fear can quickly lead to conflict and the desire to return to the old order.

This is similar to the experience of Moses. Although the Israelites initially were excited to leave the slavery of Egypt, it did not take long before many wanted to return. Behind them was slavery and death, but that was preferred to the unknown future before them. Without the strong leadership of Moses it is doubtful they would have made the transition from slavery to freedom. Likewise, it requires a strong transformational leader to help the church transition from its past to become a missional church.

TRANSFORMATIONAL LEADERS MUST LEAD

Perhaps one of the most important factors that prevent churches from experiencing transformation is pastors who don't lead.[11] Two things occur when strong leadership is absent in the church. Good leaders leave, and dysfunctional people take charge of the church.[12] Without strong leadership a church will never make the transition to becoming missional.

This will be difficult for many

> *People don't quit their organizations; they quit their leaders.*[13]
> —James M. Kouzes and Barry Z. Posner

pastors because they do not see themselves as leaders nor do they want to be leaders. George Barna surveyed Protestant pastors and found that only 12 percent identified leadership as one of their spiritual gifts. However, nearly two-thirds of them claimed the gift of teaching or preaching.[14] Unfortunately, the pastor-teacher model is not sufficient to lead a missional church.[15] Churches that successfully transition into missional communities will require pastors who have strong leadership gifts.

It is not easy for a pastor of a small church to lead the church, especially if it has a long history of rapid pastoral change. Many of the smaller churches where I live were served for many years by students at a nearby seminary. It was not unusual for these churches to have a new pastor every year or two. These churches often began to see themselves as simply a training facility for pastors to prepare them for their ministries when they completed their degree. Such a defeatist attitude is frustrating for several reasons.

Nowhere in Scripture is there a justification for any church to accept a role of training ministers for greater service elsewhere. Every church has been called into existence by God to minister to the community where He has placed it. The purpose of the church is to advance the kingdom of God, not to be a place where young preachers can practice being pastors.

This attitude also limits the church's ability to see a better future for itself. These churches have been conditioned to accept a maintenance mentality. Student pastors do not have the time, the experience, and, in many cases, the desire to lead these churches in new ways of doing ministry. Many of these students are only in the church community on Saturdays and Sundays and return to the seminary as soon as the last service ends on Sunday.

I don't want to be overly critical at this point, but I have known too many student pastors who needed a church to fulfill their seminary requirements and to help pay for their education. They knew they would not be at the church after they graduated, so they had little interest in starting new ministries or leading the church to consider a fresh vision from God. Their seminary studies limited the amount of time they could devote to new ministries, so they had little incentive to explore such ministries. The church had called them to preach at their regular services and to provide some pastoral care when members experienced problems in life. They were also expected to conduct funerals and wedding services for the members and their families. In other words, they were expected to maintain the current ministries of the church. Decades of this kind of ministry conditioned the church to expect nothing better, and they became satisfied with that.

When a church sees its ministry as merely providing a place where students can learn how to be pastors, it often demonstrates little respect for the pastor's office or leadership. In addition to the student pastors I discussed in the previous paragraph, I have also known some seminary students who wanted to serve their churches and lead them into new ministries but were unable to do so because the congregations did not respect their leadership. The lay leaders remembered too many times in the past when new pastors would recommend new ministries and then leave them about the time the ministries were implemented. The people didn't have the expertise to continue the new ministries, and the resources and effort that went into them were lost.

To protect themselves from this happening again, these congregations simply rejected any suggestions for new ministries from their young pastors. The pastors in turn soon decided to save themselves the anguish of having their ideas repeatedly shot down and stopped offering new suggestions. They slipped into a maintenance mode, looking forward to their graduation when God would call them to a place that would appreciate their ideas, and the church continued to experience the maintenance ministry to which it had become accustomed.

A small church will not move from a maintenance mentality to a missional mentality unless it has a pastor who will provide it with loving and long-term leadership. These churches are like families, reserving leadership positions to family members. A pastor has to be adopted into a family before he or she will be able to provide leadership to that family. In such a church it is not uncommon for it to take years before the pastor can finally become a leader in the church.

I was at Hebron for seven years before I was adopted into the family. Before that I was appreciated and loved, but I wasn't part of the family. I could only provide limited pastoral leadership to the church. Prior to my coming to this church, their normal pastoral tenure was about twelve months. Occasionally, a student pastor would stay eighteen to twenty-four months, but there were also times when the pastor would leave after only six months. The lay leaders in the church provided the leadership; the pastor preached sermons and visited people in the hospital. It was accepted that the pastor would not be around long enough to become part of the family. Then I was called to be the pastor.

> *The most fundamental leader-ship skill is the ability to trust and to build trust.*[16]
> —N. Graham Standish

When the church adopted me into the family in the seventh year of my pastorate, it began to trust my ministry and leadership. During a brief period of a few weeks that year two long-time members of the church shared private matters in their lives with me and allowed me to minister to them. In both cases they told me that they had never told another pastor about the things they were sharing with me. I didn't realize the significance of those words then, but I do now. They were saying they trusted me, and it was at that point that our congregation began to move forward doing some new things.

How can a small church pastor lead the church when he or she is not considered a leader by many within the church? You lead by leading the leaders. It is imperative that you identify the leaders in the church and begin to work with them to bring about the changes that need to occur. You spend time with them and point out the things that you believe could be improved. You explain the benefits to the church if those changes were made, and you help them own those changes. Do not expect these lay leaders to accept every suggestion you make, but as you continue to build relationships with them and earn their trust, you will find they will become more responsive to your recommendations. If they take ownership of your suggestions and recommend them to the church body, many of them will be accepted, and the church will begin to change.

TRANSFORMATIONAL LEADERS MUST STAY POSITIVE

One of the few questions the pastor search committee asked me came from one of the older members on the committee: "Do you think there is any hope for our church?" Spoken or not, that is the question that is on the minds of many people in our smaller churches. One of the greatest gifts a leader can give his or her church is the gift of hope. The Bible is a book that consistently proclaims hope to its readers, and our churches need to hear that message of hope. "To be true spiritual leaders, we need to be—not negative, cynical, angry, bitter, depreciative, and hopeless. Too many churches are led by angry cynics. It's no wonder that these churches are declining. Who wants to be around negative people who sap life and kill faith?"[17]

More times than I care to count people have told me they were leaving their churches because of the negativity of their pastors. These were not people who wanted to have their ears tickled with flowery, soothing messages, but they had become weary of feeling beaten up every Sunday. I have visited some of these churches and found their criticisms valid and wondered how they endured it as long as they had. I would leave those worship services wondering what had made these pastors so angry and why they remained in the ministry with the attitudes they had.

Such pastors are grace killers who should carefully consider the words of C. H. Spurgeon written over a hundred years ago in his *Lectures to My Students:*

A graceless pastor is a blind man elected to the professorship of optics, philosophizing upon light and vision, discoursing upon and distinguishing to others the nice shades and delicate blendings of the prismatic colours, while he himself is absolutely in the dark!

He is a dumb man elevated to the chair of music, a deaf man fluent upon symphonies and harmonies! He is a mole professing to educate eaglets; a limpet elevated to preside over angels. . . .

Moreover, when a preacher is poor in grace, any lasting good which may be the result of his ministry, will usually be feeble and utterly out of proportion with what may have been expected.[18]

The transformational pastor will be a messenger of grace and hope. Almost any sermon can be preached from either a negative or a positive perspective. Guess which one brings life to the listeners! Every day you will choose the attitude with which you will live and minister. A negative, condemning attitude will not inspire your congregation to follow you. Every day you will choose how you will see your congregation. You can choose to see their faults and problems, or you can choose to see their essential goodness. Just remember—if they were perfect people, they may not have settled on you for their pastor!

> *The focus of leadership always has to be on people's essential goodness, the good that they do, their possibilities, and God's presence is with us in everything.*[19]
>
> —N. Graham Standish

Many times during my ministry at Hebron I reminded the congregation that I had much more confidence in them than most of them had in themselves. I knew in my heart what we could accomplish when we trusted God. People tend to gravitate to the expectations others have of them, and congregations are no exception. I had very high expectations of our people, and they seldom disappointed me. In fact, they consistently achieved far more than most would have thought possible. When they did not, it was not for a lack of effort or faith, it was the result of poor leadership on my part.

TRANSFORMATIONAL LEADERS MUST LOVE THE PEOPLE THEY LEAD

One of the main problems facing smaller churches is poor self-esteem.[20] Such churches often feel like second-class citizens in the kingdom of God. They don't feel very desirable and may wonder why any pastor would be interested in serving them. One of the questions they need to have answered is, "Pastor, do you love us?"

In larger churches this may not be as much of an issue, but the smaller church exists as a family. It is important that family members care for one another, and until they are convinced the pastor truly loves them, he or she cannot become part of the family.

The story is told of a woman who sued her husband of thirty years for divorce. As they stood before the judge, he asked why she was seeking a divorce after so many years of marriage. She responded that she could not stay married to a man who did not love her, and she was convinced he didn't because he hadn't told her he loved her in years. Her husband was shocked and responded, "Maggie, I told you on the day we married that I loved you. I would have told you if I changed my mind!"

Marriages remain strong when the partners regularly declare and show their love to each other. The same is true in pastor-church relationships. Your congregation needs to hear you tell them how much you love them and enjoy being their pastor. They need to see your words confirmed by your actions and attitudes, and if you can't love the people you serve, it would probably be best if you moved on. They will not follow a pastor into the kind of transformation this book is describing unless they are convinced that pastor loves them.

TRANSFORMATIONAL LEADERS MUST BE RISK TAKERS

One of my favorite Bible stories is how Abram was willing to take a step of faith and begin a journey with an unknown destination. God challenged Abram to leave his family and to go "to a land that I will show you" (Gen. 12:1). When Abram began his journey, he didn't know whether to take his first step to the north, east, south, or west because God was not going to show him where he was going until he began the journey.

Transformational change is very much like starting a journey with an unknown destination. Although you may have a general idea of where you are going, the final destination is likely to be different than you imagined.

> *I think that a compelling vision combined with a unique ability to manage risk is the magic behind successful entrepreneurs.*[21]
> —Warren Bennis

In fact, you will probably find there really isn't a final destination. As changes begin to occur in the church, other needed changes will be identified; and as our world continues to experience change, it will demand even more changes in the missional church.

Abram had to leave the stability of his family with its wealth and prestige and journey to a distant land. There was great risk involved, but somehow he knew that there was greater risk in refusing the journey. As noted briefly in chapter 1, "Missional leaders are risk takers. This characteristic does not imply that missional leaders do not consider potential consequences of their actions. They do consider those consequences, but they also consider the risks associated with *not* taking action."[22]

Another risk associated with transformational change is that it is often messy. Most of our churches are stuck in their ruts, and although we may complain about them, they do provide us with a sense of security and peace. As long as we stay in our maintenance ruts, we know what is expected of us and we have a pretty good sense of what is going to happen. There are seldom any surprises in our worship services, our committee work, or the programs we have always offered. However, transformational change isn't so neat. In fact, there will be times of great chaos that will cause most of us to wish for the "good old days" when everything was done decently and in order.

Effective leaders today reside somewhere between absolute order and absolute chaos. The trick is to ride the wave of chaos to its crest without becoming engulfed by it. Instead of seeking order, leaders count the chaos. The worst thing leaders can do today is to avoid the chaos of the moment for the order of the past. To do so signs one's death warrant as a leader and consigns the organization to death.[23]

As great as the risks associated with leading a small church to a missional mind-set are, the risks are even greater if such transformation does not occur. We see all around us the results of small churches remaining maintenance-minded. The congregation grows older, less and less ministry is done in the community, and the congregation cries out for growth while refusing to change anything that would allow such growth to occur. Good, godly people become filled with a sense of hopelessness and helplessness as they see their church slowly dying around them.

TRANSFORMATIONAL LEADERS MUST HAVE A VISION

Although we will talk elsewhere about the importance of a vision for a missional church, effective leaders must first possess a personal vision. Mike Regele states this well:

We need leaders who are driven by moral vision.

A visionary leader is a leader who is driven by a clear image of an ideal condition, a condition that does not satisfactorily exist. It is a vision of what ought to be in the lives of people, in contrast with what is. It imagines people living free and wholly alive in a world where peace and justice prevail for all persons, not just the self or a privileged class. The disparity between "what is" and "what ought to be" generates passion in the heart of the leader. A passion in the soul compels him or her to transform this vision into reality. Such passion has a distinctly moral quality to it.[24]

Few churches have a clear sense of vision for their ministry, and much of that blame must lie with their pastor, because few pastors with whom I have spoken have a clear vision of what their church should look like. There are exceptions, and it is exciting to talk to a pastor who has a clear vision for his or her church. Such pastors are enthusiastic and passionate about their vision, and they can't help but talk about it. Un-

> *Pastors who lead congregations to find a corporate vision [have] a personal vision already at work in their lives.*[25]
> —Ron Crandall

fortunately, in my experience these exceptions are rare. When I ask most pastors to tell me their vision for their church, they confess they don't have one. As one pastor said to me once, "I'm just not very good with this vision thing."

Such pastors are going through the motions of pastoral ministry. They may be very proficient at what they do, but they lack passion and enthusiasm. Because these qualities are contagious, if the pastor doesn't possess them, it is unlikely many in the church will either. Church guests quickly pick up on the lack of passion and enthusiasm and make a mental note that this is probably not a church to which they will return, and the congregation wonders why they can't keep the new people who visit their church.

Of all the items discussed in this chapter, having a vision is the most important requirement for a transformational leader. If the pastor does not have a vision for where the church needs to go, the other things really won't matter that much. The transformation to becoming a missional church is unlikely to happen unless the pastor clearly understands where God wants to lead the church.

TRANSFORMATIONAL LEADERS MUST COMMUNICATE

It is not enough to have a vision; that vision must be communicated to the congregation until it becomes their vision. Transformational leaders understand that a person cannot overcommunicate, especially when that person is trying to lead change in an organization. Rick Warren insists that "vision and purpose must be restated every twenty-six days to keep the church moving in the right direction."[27] Max DePree has "learned that if you are a leader and you're not sick and tired of communicating, you probably aren't doing a good enough job."[28] If the vision is not constantly kept before the people, it is unlikely they will own the vision and even more unlikely the vision will ever be implemented.

You cannot be a poor communicator and a good leader.[26]
—Henry and Richard Blackaby

When I work with a larger church seeking transformation, we usually work with the leadership of the church. This includes staff, board members, and members of various committees or teams within the church. However, when a small church asks me to help them in transformation, it is vital that we invite the entire congregation to be a part of the process. This again reflects the family atmosphere of the smaller congregation, and it is important that the entire family be involved in any changes that might be occurring within the family.

It is also important to remember that communication must be a two-way conversation. We no longer live in a time where an authority figure can stand before the people he or she leads and announce some grand new direction the organization is taking. It is arrogant on the part of any leader to assume that he or she will get the vision exactly right. Successful business leaders in the twenty-first century know they need to listen to their employees because employees often can spot flaws in a new strategic plan that the leaders did not see. Church leaders need to learn the same lesson. The communication that is required must include opportunities for feedback from everyone in the smaller church, and leaders must ensure that persons sharing feedback know they have been heard and their thoughts considered even if their suggestions are not implemented.

Anytime leaders are communicating the vision, they must keep in mind the relational nature of the smaller church. Glenn Daman reminds us that "to develop ownership . . . any change or goal must be couched in the context of relationships. The vision needs to relate to the needs of friends, family, and neighbors so people can see how the vision will strengthen these relationships rather than just build the organization."[29] To speak only of growing the church or creating new programs is unlikely to stir the passions of many people in smaller churches, but to speak specifically of how the new vision will impact their families and friends will be received much more warmly.

When communicating the need to change, it is important to communicate positive messages. Early in my pastorate I learned the hard way that if a person communicates from a negative perspective, it is much more likely to create resistance. People feel threatened. They feel that the way they have been serving God is being questioned. After reading one book on church transformation a pastor recently told me that she felt the author was saying that everything she had ever done in ministry was wrong. She was frustrated and somewhat angry. People in our congregations will feel the same way if they believe we are saying that their previous ministries have been ineffective.

It is much better to affirm the positive impact the church has had over the years while encouraging the congregation that it is time to look at making their ministries even better. I like to remind churches that any changes that might be recommended are to replace programs and ministries that were probably resisted when they were first proposed. The ministries that people often fight to preserve were probably just as fiercely resisted when they were first suggested at an earlier time in the church's history. However, the church did adapt them, and they served the church and community well for many years, but now it may be time to replace them with other ministries that will better address the needs of people today. When leaders affirm the previous ministries of the church, people are more likely to listen to suggested changes that will take the church to a higher place of service to their families and friends.

Leaders must also communicate clearly. I challenge churches to work on their vision statement until it will fit on a T-shirt. The statement itself should be concise enough so that anyone in the church, including children, can repeat it. It is just as important that the meaning of the vision and the reasons behind it be clearly explained until they are understood and owned by the congregation. Members of a small church are not going to be interested in transforming into a missional community until they clearly understand what that means and how that is going to impact their church and community. It is critical that they have not only an unclouded picture of what this will look like but also a clear understanding of the process that will enable this to occur.[31] Without such clarity they will continue to resist any change. This is another reason why it is so important for communication to include feedback. When feedback is encouraged, it allows people to clear up any confusion they may have about the vision or the process.

> *When the same message comes at people from six different directions, it stands a better chance of being heard and remembered, on both intellectual and emotional levels.*[30]
>
> —John Kotter

Every means available to the church leadership should be used for communicating the vision. This includes sermons, small-group gatherings, individual meetings with parishioners, bulletins, church newsletters, and mass mailings to the church membership. It also includes some communication tools that smaller churches may not normally use.

E-mail is a fast, inexpensive, and effective means of communicating with a congregation. Although it is an important communication tool in the twenty-first century, it should not be the only tool used, especially in smaller churches. The first rule in communicating with smaller churches is to remember the importance of relationships. E-mail can be a very impersonal avenue of communication, especially for persons who receive dozens of e-mails each day. Use e-mail, but don't make this your primary communication tool.

Another tool not used by many smaller churches is a church Web site. This can be a very effective means of communicating with the congregation and with the community. One survey of over 1,300 congregations that have Web sites and use e-mail reported that 83 percent of those churches said their use of the Internet improved the life of their churches.[32] However, smaller churches seldom see the benefits that a church Web site can provide. A study by Ellison Research found that only 29 percent of churches with fewer than 100 people in the congregation have a Web site.[33]

Many small churches will claim that having a Web site is too expensive and is only for larger churches. However, there are now a number of Web site development tools such as Microsoft Publisher that are very inexpensive and will enable almost anyone to develop an attractive Web site. There are also several companies that will host the site for a very small monthly fee. The American Bible Society is committed to providing every church a free donor-supported Web site. Their sites are attractive and would be a good way for a smaller church to begin their Internet presence. They even provide a free Web Builder tool kit that makes developing the site a simple task.[34]

The Web site can be used to keep the vision before the people and to let the surrounding community know what is happening in the church. Even nonmembers can be attracted to a church's vision that touches their hearts, and this can be an entry point for them into the church. It is a communication tool that no church can ignore today.

Another important communication tool seldom found in smaller churches is a blog. A blog can be included as part of the church's Web site, or it can be a stand-alone blog. It is possible to create a free blog in a matter of minutes and have it posted on the Internet for the entire world to view.[35] This is a great way for the pastor or other church leaders to share the vision with the church and to obtain feedback from readers. Not only can members of the congregation be encouraged to read the blog regularly to keep up with changes in the church, but others may read it as well. Some may even post some helpful comments that church members never considered. These comments may add great value to the vision and cause it to grow beyond the original thinking of the church leaders.

There is another benefit blogs provide smaller churches. They can expand the ministry of a smaller church far beyond its geographical area. Persons anywhere in the world can access a blog on the Internet, allowing the church an opportunity to minister to people in every nation. Not only can a blog provide church members a means to dialogue with one another about their vision, but a blog can also enable the church to share its witness around the world twenty-four hours a day. That is being missional!

TRANSFORMATIONAL LEADERS MUST DEVELOP TEAMS

I recently met with a church's search committee as they began their search for a new pastor. One of the things I requested during my first meeting with the committee is that they tell me the strengths and weaknesses of their previous pastor. The committee was very complimentary of their former pastor. He was very talented and had provided good leadership to this church for nearly a decade. They could identify few things they wish he had done better, but they did identify one. He did nearly everything himself.

This is a growing church with an average attendance of well over a hundred people each Sunday morning. It is a church with a secretary and an associate minister, and yet the pastor was still preparing the church bulletin each week. The committee said that the pastor felt he had to attend every committee meeting and be involved in every decision made in the church. When I asked why he felt that way, they believed that it was because he came from a much smaller church where he had become accustomed to doing everything and that he had not been able to break that mind-set.

As mentioned earlier, working with a team is an important quality of missional leadership. So it will be essential for a leader to develop a team of adult leaders before trying to turn a maintenance church into a missional church. Bill Easum believes that one of the major mistakes turnaround pastors make is the failure to develop a team before starting the turnaround process.[36] In larger churches that team will likely be paid staff people, but in smaller churches your team will consist of spiritually mature lay leaders who are often seeking ways to better serve their church and their Lord. One of the most important things a new pastor can do when starting his or her ministry at a church is to begin to identify these people and start investing additional time in them to see if they are people who can help lead the church in this transformational process.

There are several reasons why a leadership team is important to a successful transformation. One is that different people have different gifts. As a pastor I had certain gifts God had given me for ministry, and my best work occurred when I was exercising those gifts. Leadership works best when you maximize your strengths and find ways to manage around your weaknesses.[37] One of the best ways to manage around your weaknesses is to bring people onto your team who are gifted in the areas where you are the weakest.

Other organizations do this. Our son was a left-handed pitcher who wanted to play college ball. One of the schools we visited his senior year was interested in him but already had several young pitchers. They were saving their scholarships for position players to replace those who were graduating. The coach understood the weaknesses his team had and was focused on adding players who could make the team stronger. We continued to visit colleges and soon found one that was willing to invest a scholarship in a pitcher.

No pastor can be a perfect preacher, prophet, teacher, pastoral caregiver, missionary, administrator, mentor, counselor, model, and spiritual guide all at the same time. God simply doesn't give everyone every gift. God calls us as leaders to a specific ministry focus. We have to lead out of the gifts we have been given and trust God to take care of the rest.[38]

A team can also help us listen to the congregation and gauge their readiness to move through the transformation process. Timing is critical in transformational work. Trying to move a congregation before they are ready will result in opposition and unnecessary struggle. Waiting too long after a congregation is ready frustrates the congregation and destroys any sense of urgency they may have had about the importance of change. A wise pastor will not trust only his or her ability to gauge a congregation's readiness but will involve the listening and discerning skills of others in the church.[39] A team can be a valuable ally in this discernment.

The team will provide vital assistance when the church is ready to implement the changes identified as critical to the achievement of God's vision for the church. It will be very hard for a pastor to continue doing pastoral duties and implement these changes alone. Either necessary pastoral ministry will be left undone or the implementation of the change will be held up. In both cases, the church suffers. But when the pastor has gathered a team, there are other people who can share in these tasks.

TRANSFORMATIONAL LEADERS MUST BE SPIRITUAL LEADERS

Famed preacher Robert Murray M'Cheyne once said, "The people's greatest need is my personal holiness. . . . A man is what he is on his knees and nothing more."[40] An effective transformational leader must first be a person of spiritual maturity. God called each of us to be something before He called us to do something. Our ministries must flow out of a deep relationship with God. We are called to be disciples, men and women who spend time with God, studying His Word, listening to His voice, and growing deeper in our relationship with Him. Such discipleship does not come except to those willing to live disciplined lives.

Personal transformation comes when our relationship with God is not just one part of our lives. Personal transformation is fueled when Jesus becomes a dynamic, ongoing presence every moment we live. Integrating the classic disciplines of Christianity into our hours, days, and weeks fosters this kind of relationship. Leaders must develop the capacity to set boundaries on the things that drain their vitality and establish space for the things that nourish the soul and renew the mind.[41]

Eugene Peterson writes about the "unbusy pastor" who refuses to crowd the day with "conspicuous activity."[42] Is it possible to be such a pastor? Yes, and we must become this type of pastor if we are to grow deeper in our own lives and be able, with integrity, to challenge our congregation to grow deeper in theirs.

To live such a life will require much discipline on our part. We will have to reserve sufficient time to pray, to study the Scriptures, and to seek God. We will have to refuse some activities suggested by others that would gain their approval in order to have the time to invest in our personal spiritual growth. This will be difficult for pastors who enjoy the applause of others for a job well done, and I confess that I am often included in that number, but unless we are willing to adopt this lifestyle, our personal transformation will be stunted as will our effectiveness as transformational leaders.

> *The focal point of any ministry is godliness. Ministry is, and always must be, an overflow of a godly life.*[43]
>
> —Irvin A. Busenitz

John Maxwell's "law of buy-in" teaches us that people must buy into their leader before they will buy into the vision.[44] In the church few things influence this willingness to buy into the leader more than his or her character. They rightfully expect their leaders to be growing deeper in their relationship with God and to be persons of integrity.

FOUR

Capturing God's Vision

Attach every change initiative to a clear purpose or goal. Change for change's sake is stupid and enervating.[1]

—Jack Welch

By now you are probably wondering when we are going to finally discuss the changes that need to occur in the church, but it is still too early to ask that question. The real question that must be answered first is, Where is God leading your church? What is God's vision for your church? Until you know where you are going, you cannot know what has to change to allow you to get there. To confuse this issue even more, until you know who you are, you cannot know where you are going. This chapter will help you discover the identity of your church and begin a process of discerning God's vision for the church. Only after doing these two things can you know what changes may be needed.

THEOLOGY

In my previous books I did not explore the theological and spiritual elements of ministry. I assumed the readers already had a grasp of those matters and were seeking more practical information. I fear my assumption was misplaced. After working with many churches and ministers during the past six years, I have found much theological confusion and, even worse, a general apathy toward theology itself.

We in ministerial leadership often seek the quick fix, the program that is guaranteed to grow our churches, the worship format that will attract all ages while alienating none, the pied piper of youth leaders who will draw all the youth of the area to our churches. Our Christian bookstores are filled with books designed to provide exactly what we are seeking. I join Anthony Robinson in his concern that most books focusing on healthy, growing churches discuss "systems theory, leadership studies, conflict management, and a variety of other approaches . . . but little that is explicitly theological or biblical in nature."[2]

Skilled at cutting through the fog, Leonard Sweet asks the church questions we would often prefer not to consider:

The church has tried everything except the one thing that is needed. It has tried to be an inclusive church. It has tried to be a confessional church. It has tried to be a program-driven church. It has tried to be a purpose-driven church. It has tried to be a seeker-sensitive church. . . . What if it tried to be a spiritual church?[3]

Perhaps one of the greatest transformations that could occur in the church would be the recovery of a sound theological belief system. Elton Trueblood once observed that many of our institutions have been severed from their roots. He referred to them as "cut-flower" institutions. While they may be beautifully arranged and set in an expensive vase, they will eventually die because they have been cut off from their roots. They cannot access the water and nutrients they need in order to live.[4] Jeffrey Jones reminds us, "In times of great change, in times when the old answers just don't work any more, the most important thing we can do is to go back to our roots."[5]

Many of our churches have beautiful buildings that provide wonderful worship presentations. They develop strong programs to reach out to their communities and hire charismatic leaders to implement those programs. Their ministries run like well-oiled machines, and the CEO-pastors and boards keep a close eye on the bottom line. However, these churches are at great risk of becoming just like the withered, dying little church down the road if they do not remain connected to their theological roots. Ellen Charry, a professor at Princeton Theological Seminary, notes that many of her students see the church as a "voluntary not-for-profit organization run like a local franchise."[6] Disconnected from their theological roots, churches will remain confused about their identity and purpose, and they will decline and eventually die regardless of how well organized and led they may be.

This disconnection is disastrous for at least a couple of reasons. A congregation's identity is found in its theological understanding. Without a strong theological understanding of what the congregation believes and who they are, there will always be confusion about their purpose and mission. Second, people want theological certainty in their churches. Thom Rainer's research of formerly unchurched people found they "were not just interested in the facts of the doctrine: they were insistent that the churches should be uncompromising in their stand."[7] Colleen Carroll spent a year researching the return of young people to Christianity and found they were seeking theological foundations for their lives.

In a pluralistic culture where all belief systems demand respect but none takes precedence, young orthodox Christians often gravitate to faith communities that send a clear message about what they believe. Campus fellowships with a blunt evangelistic bent consistently attract more members than mainline groups that lack a distinct identity or hesitate to proclaim the universality of the gospel message.[8]

What is the theological identity of your church? In our postmodern times the old terms such as "conservative," "fundamentalist," "liberal," "moderate," "evangelical," and "orthodox" probably have little meaning to most people. We live in a time when we feel we have to hyphenate everything in order to explain it. To simply refer to your church with one of the theological descriptors used in the modern period would probably not catch its true identity. I would probably refer to myself as a conservative evangelical, but what in the world does that mean? However, the church I pastored for twenty years knew what I believed, and they knew what they believed.

Just as the identity of our church was wrapped up very tightly in our theology, so is the identity of your church if it is clear about what it believes. Clearly understanding its theological identity is vital for a church that desires to be on mission with God.

CORE VALUES

One of the most interesting exercises I do with a small church is to lead it through a process of discovering its core values. More often than not when I suggest doing this, the church leaders will respond that they know who and what their church is, but if they agree to go through the process, they usually learn some new things about their church. It is absolutely essential for any church wanting to engage in transformational ministry to clearly understand the core values that drive its decision-making processes.[10]

> *More than what is stated, what is done reveals purpose. Actions speak louder than words.*[9]
> —Milfred Minatrea

The core values of a church determine its decisions. The behaviors, the attitudes, and the decisions made by individuals and groups are always determined by their core values. A church will sometimes list a certain value as one of its core values when in reality it is nothing more than wishful thinking, that is, a value the church thinks should be a core value. The true core values of a church will be seen in the church's ministries, decisions, and budgets.

One night I was helping a church identify its core values. At the end of the evening we were posting the core values the congregation believed defined their church. One of those core values was youth. When I wrote it on the board, a woman spoke up and asked, "If youth are a core value in this church, why am I the only one who is willing to work with the youth? Why is it that no one will help me even when I ask?" The room became very silent as we discussed the difference between the core values that actually exist in a church and those values people think should exist in a church. This congregation began a conversation that should have occurred years before but didn't until they were challenged about something they believed was a priority in their church but actually was not.

Almost every congregation I work with claims they want their church to grow numerically. They say they want to reach new people for Christ. Yet an examination of their ministries and budgets makes it obvious that everything that occurs in the church is for the current members. One small church had a 2006 budget of $50,000. Three hundred dollars of that money was earmarked for outreach. I know this church, and the people would insist that they want to reach out to their community, but their budget does not reflect that to be one their core values. I also know that a few years before this their total budget was less than $50,000, but they had over $3,000 budgeted for outreach. I don't know what changed, but I do know that when stated core values conflict with the actual practices of a church, those practices are the true core values of that church.

Tom Bandy offers a good tool to help a church identify its core values.[11] It is a fun exercise I use with churches that seems to work very well. The process helps a church narrow down a lengthy list of values to the three or four core values that give the church a better understanding of who it is.

BEDROCK BELIEFS

The next piece of a church's identity is found in the church's bedrock beliefs. Tom Bandy defines bedrock beliefs as "the principles or symbols of faith that matter most in the daily life of congregational participants. It is to these principles or symbols that participants immediately turn to in times of crisis."[12] Like core values, every church has certain bedrock beliefs that sustain it during times of difficulty. This is also true for individuals.

One night I was leading a congregation in an exercise to determine their bedrock beliefs, and I suddenly became aware of mine. It is Jesus' promise that He would never leave us nor forsake us. I do not enjoy flying, and I realized that evening that every time I've ever boarded an airplane that verse has run through my mind like a recording reminding me of God's presence. I also remembered the day I was in the "holding area" of a hospital waiting my turn for surgery. What I really wanted to do was crawl off that gurney and go home. Again, I was sustained by this promise of God's presence.

A couple in the church I pastored lost everything when their house burned to the ground a few years before I came to that church. They often spoke of how the church not only helped them rebuild their house but also helped them rebuild their lives after that loss. One of the husband's bedrock beliefs was that the church would be there anytime he faced a difficult time in his life.

Just as an individual's bedrock beliefs shape his or her life, so does a church's bedrock beliefs shape the life of its congregation. Bandy also provides a useful exercise to help a church determine its bedrock beliefs, which I often use when working with churches.[13] I would suggest that a congregation bring someone in from the outside to lead them through these exercises. This person could be a denominational leader, a consultant or coach, or another trusted pastor from the community.

VISION

Once the church understands its core values and bedrock beliefs, it will better understand its identity. Only then is it ready to discern God's vision for it. Clearly understanding this vision is essential for any successful ministry in the church. I believe this so strongly that I will make an even bolder statement: If a church does not have a clear, God-given vision that directs its ministry, it will eventually die. In my experiences working with smaller churches I find very few that have a clear vision for ministry. These churches exist today because of an earlier vision that provided them direction and allowed them to grow. However, these churches lost any sense of vision long ago and now drift along to a certain death, irrelevant to most people around them.

> *A vision from God has the potential to turn a maintenance mentality into a ministry mentality.*[14]
>
> —Aubrey Malphurs

George Barna offers one definition of vision: "Vision for ministry is a clear mental image of a preferable future imparted by God to His chosen servants and is based upon an accurate understanding of God, self and circumstances."[15] Let's briefly unpack this definition.

A vision should be more than an idea but should be seen in your mind's eye. You should be able to see what the results would look like if this vision was fulfilled.

It is a preferred future, and this is one of the exciting things about a vision. Too often our churches simply drift along responding to the circumstances occurring around them. A vision enables the church to prepare its future. You have a much better chance of enjoying success when you determine your own future, and a vision allows you to do that because it keeps you focused on what God has called you to do rather than being tossed about by the events happening around you.

A vision is imparted by God. It doesn't really matter what the pastor, the deacons, the elders, or the denomination believe the vision of the church should be. It must be God's vision for the church that we seek because only His vision really matters.

Some Christian leaders seem to believe that in our postmodern era change occurs so quickly that a church cannot determine or define the future. I disagree. In fact, times of great change are when a church, or any organization, either must define its future or find itself blown around by every change that happens. This is especially important for the smaller church with fewer resources. Such churches must have a clear vision of where God is leading them and the ministries they should be providing.

To say that God cannot lead us to a clear vision of a preferred future for our churches is to say that God is not sovereign and omniscient. If we believe that He knows all things, then we have to believe that He knows the changes that are coming to our churches and communities and how our churches can best minister in that new world. Why should it be difficult to believe that He can prepare the church in advance for those changes?

This vision will be imparted to God's chosen servants. This does not mean that God only speaks to the pastor or to certain leaders in the church. A vision can come from anyone in the church and, in some cases, from someone outside the church. God's vision for the church may come through a person who has left its fellowship for one reason or another. We have to be very sensitive to how God may choose to speak to us, and we must be careful that we not refuse to hear God's vision from someone we believe may not be one of God's "chosen servants."

THE DIFFERENCE BETWEEN VISION AND MISSION

The question is often asked about the difference between mission and vision. For a more detailed look at mission statements I refer the reader to my previous book *The Healthy Small Church*.[16] Here we just need to point out that the mission statement is a broad statement about what the church should be doing. The vision statement describes how the church will live out its mission in this present day and time. A vision will change as the circumstances change. The mission will never be fully completed, but a vision can be achieved. Then a new vision will emerge to direct the ministry of the church in new directions.

> *The church has more than enough mission statements and not nearly enough mission relationships and mission movements.*[17]
>
> —Leonard Sweet

While the church's mission is rather broad, its vision should be very narrow. The purpose of a vision is to focus the ministries of the church on the specific tasks God has given it for this time in the life of the church. Any vision statement that is longer than two or three sentences is probably too broad. One denomination recently went through a year-long process to determine its vision, and when they finished, they had a statement that was several paragraphs long. The document they developed described their mission, but they certainly had not discerned God's vision for the denomination, and they had no more focus than when they started the process. Truly determining God's vision for a ministry is to focus on the specific purposes and ministries God has given your church for this specific time and place.

> *A church must know why it exists to know what it is supposed to do.*[18]
>
> —Thom Rainer

DISCERNING GOD'S VISION

When I work with church members in a visioning process, I begin by helping them identify their core values and bedrock beliefs as discussed earlier. The work is divided into two sessions, and each session requires two to three hours depending on how many questions they have as we complete each one. We then schedule a visioning retreat that lasts an entire Saturday. Even if the church pastor leads the two sessions, it is probably best to bring in someone from outside the church for the visioning retreat. While there are many ways to discern a vision, I will share the exercise I often use with churches. Other leaders in our region use a very similar process when they work with their churches.

I begin by defining "vision" and explaining the difference between "vision" and "mission." We then discuss the discernment process. Discernment is something we seldom practice in our modern churches. Many small churches are more likely to want to try something that worked well in another church than to spend the time to discern God's unique vision for themselves. Those of us in pastoral ministry are perhaps even guiltier. We go off to a conference hosted by some well-known church leader, hear how he or she led a church in some great ministry, buy the materials, and return to our church determined to duplicate that success. It's a lot easier to try to adapt someone else's vision than doing the hard work of praying, seeking God, and discerning His vision for our church and its future ministry. Unfortunately, such adaptation usually doesn't produce the results we seek because we are trying to do something that is not God's plan for our church.

After discussing the discernment process I give them a list of scriptures and ask them to go off by themselves for thirty minutes, read three of the passages, and begin to reflect on them using these questions:

- Who are we?
- What is our purpose?
- What is God calling us to do?
- What will we do to answer God's calling?
- What reflections can you share when you are again with your small group?

When the thirty minutes are up, we ask the participants to return to their tables and begin to share their discoveries with one another. It is all right if they haven't answered all the questions before they return, because they will get a chance to answer them during this discussion.

By now it is usually time to break for lunch, which we eat at the church. During mealtime this conversation often continues. For many churches, this is the longest the church members have talked about these questions, and it usually generates a lot of energy and insight.

Following the meal it is time for more reflection. Again they are sent off by themselves for thirty minutes to prayerfully consider two more questions:

- What do you think God's vision is for your church?
- Where do you think God is leading your congregation?

When this time has passed, we bring everyone back together to discuss their findings with the whole group. As people begin to share, I write their comments down on an easel pad so everyone can see them. We begin to look for a pattern. Are a number of people hearing the same thing? Does God seem to be leading this church in a particular direction? In my experience there are three possible things that can occur at this point.

One congregation worked through this process very well. It became rather obvious that God was leading them in a certain direction when one person began to speak about how earlier efforts to do ministry had been halted by conflict in the church. It became even more obvious that although the conflict happened many years ago, there was a pattern of conflict existing in the church that had never been addressed. As I watched the pastor who had been there less than one year, it was clear that this was the first time he heard of these problems. The process we had followed seemed to give them permission to discuss something they had preferred to ignore for many years. While there was no clear vision discerned that day, the process did allow the church to begin talking about problems that had to be addressed before they could enjoy a more productive ministry.

Another congregation that followed this process seemed to discern a clear vision from God. Their core values, bedrock beliefs, and the discernment process seemed to lead them to focus their ministry on families in the area, and specifically, to single-parent homes. The church members did not leave the visioning retreat with a clear sense of what that ministry would look like, but they did leave with the conviction that ministering to the children and single-parent homes in their rural community was the vision God was giving them. This church with an average attendance of about forty people now has a more focused ministry designed to meet a critical need that exists in its community.

A third result I see from these retreats is that the church members need more time to process their thoughts. Actually, a clear vision often does not come at the end of the visioning retreat. What does occur is that the members now have a common language they can use as they continue to seek that vision. They now talk about things they may not have even considered important before. It makes them more tuned into what God may be saying to them.

THE IMPACT OF A VISION

Most churches I know, both small and large, are focused primarily on maintenance. They budget and develop programs based on what their members want. They pay lip service to those outside the church, but the vast majority of their resources are spent on those already inside. The church just drifts along from Sunday to Sunday and from year to year and wonders why people aren't knocking down the doors trying to get in. Drifting will get a church into trouble.

A few years ago my wife and I owned a bass boat. I was a bivocational pastor working in a factory that had a bass club, and we enjoyed fishing in the Saturday tournaments sponsored by the club. One of the things I realized was that the only time I ever really got into trouble on the water was when I was drifting in the boat. The Ohio River is near our home, and I would take the boat down to the river to fish. Sometimes I would run the boat up the river and allow it to drift down, driven by the river's current, while I fished the riverbanks. One day my motor became hung in a tree that had fallen into the river. Although I could not see the tree or the branches, they had wrapped themselves around my motor. I could not start the motor without breaking the prop, and the water was too shallow to use my trolling motor. I had to push the boat backward against the current to free it from the branches. I was stuck there for nearly an hour.

Another time the boat drifted onto a submerged rock where the motor became stuck. This particular boat did not have power tilt and trim, so I could not raise the motor off the rock. I went to the front of the boat and began to rock back and forth hoping to break free from the rock. Suddenly, I lost my balance, and while I did not fall into the river, I did fall into the boat, breaking six rods and getting three treble hooks stuck in my arms.

Not once did I ever get into trouble fishing either when I had the motor running or when I used the trolling motor. When I was operating one of those motors, I was moving with purpose and toward a destination. It was only when I allowed myself to drift that I found myself in trouble. The same is true of churches.

A church that is merely drifting through life is a church that will encounter problems and is unlikely to accomplish anything of significance. Churches that have a clear direction and purpose to their ministries are the ones that will have the greatest impact for the kingdom of God.

One tremendous benefit of leaning on God's vision is that the church ceases to be a victim of circumstances. Pulsating with the belief that He has directed the ministry to pursue specific outcomes, the laity exhibit a renewed interest in and commitment to ministry. Believing that God is involved in their efforts, they become more aggressive at creating the desired future rather than waiting for that imagined scenario to happen. Instead of simply reacting to conditions, the people begin to formulate their own ministry environment by anticipating changes and fostering a world that enables them to be effective.[19]

Is that what you want for your church? Are you tired of seeing your church merely drifting along, barely surviving, and having little impact on the community God has given you to reach? Discovering God's vision can be a launching pad for your church to enter an exciting new chapter of ministry. That vision will help you identify the ministry God wants to provide through your church to your community.

> *Vision isn't everything, but it's the beginning of everything.*[20]
> —David McAllister-Wilson

FINDING YOUR NICHE

In southeastern Indiana it seems that we have a Baptist church on every road. In chapter 2 I mentioned that as our family moved around the county in which we lived, we would join the Baptist church in the new community, but nothing ever really changed. Each church was basically a carbon copy of every other church in our denomination. That really hasn't changed much in the past five decades. One of the questions I like to ask congregations is why anyone would want to come to their church. If every church offers essentially the same worship experiences and the same programs, then it really doesn't matter which church a person attends. I then challenge these churches to seek a fresh vision from God that will include a target audience for their ministry.

When I ask smaller churches who they would most like to reach, the majority respond that they want to reach young families with small children. The problem is that if every church is trying to reach this group, the churches that will be the most successful will be the ones with the most resources and programs to attract these young families. That is unlikely to include many smaller churches. However, in every community there are other potential recipients of the ministry of a church that no other church is intentionally reaching out to.

A number of years ago a pastor of a large church in Texas told an evangelism conference that the church he pastored had spent several months trying to identify a group of people that no other church in their community was trying to reach. They finally identified such a group of people. No church in that large city was reaching out to the divorced people in their city. Their church developed a ministry to do that, and he reported that as he looked out on the three worship services each Sunday morning, he was looking at 700 people who had come into their church through that one ministry.

> *Churches must discover their unique little niches. Their survival depends upon it.*[21]
> —Robert Nash Jr.

Another pastor recently told me that two women in his church had started a ministry to women and families who had lost a baby or small child. One of the women had experienced such a loss herself, and she remembered the pain and the loneliness she felt during that period in her life. These two laywomen developed this ministry and brought it to their pastor. The church is now providing some resources to assist them, and it is already having a positive impact in their community.

A pastor of a small church is praying about starting a ministry for people who have been hurt by the church. Unfortunately, she should have no shortage of people to reach out to. Her goal is to make their church a safe, inviting place for those who have been wounded by the church. Any small church that developed such an emphasis might not stay small for very long.

A denominational leader was leading a workshop on church growth when he asked the participants who their churches were trying to reach. He soon filled the chalkboard with the answers. One group was conspicuously missing from the list: senior adults. No church represented in that workshop had any specific ministry to minister to the older citizens of its community. The misperception may be that older adults are either already Christians or have no interest in becoming Christians. The reality is that they may be out of church for a number of possible reasons and would return to the church that showed an interest in them. It may also be true that even if they have not been interested in spiritual things in the past, as they reach the end of their lives, they may have some questions about life and eternity they would love to have answered.

These are just a few potential people groups that exist in every community on which few churches have intentionally focused their ministries, and this list is certainly not exhaustive. God may want to use your church to reach out to one of these groups or some other group within your community. Developing such a ministry would set your church apart from the other smaller churches in your area and enable you to direct your limited resources to a specific group of people who need to experience God in their lives. Only by earnestly seeking God's vision for your church will you know who He wants you to reach out to, and it is in that reaching out that your church becomes more missional in its thinking and in its ministry.

FIVE

FAQs About Change

What is the number-one issue facing Christian organizations on the North American continent today? . . . The need to initiate and implement planned change from within an organization.[1]

—Lyle Schaller

The story is told of a new pastor preaching his first sermon in a small church. He spoke of his vision for the church, and he spoke of his passion to lead the church into the twentieth century. A deacon sitting near the front whispered loudly to the pastor, "Pastor, this is the twenty-first century." The pastor quickly responded, "One century at a time."

Because our culture is constantly changing, it is safe to say that the church should always be in a state of change. Many small churches have ministries that served them well in the mid-twentieth century, but this is a new century. As we saw in an earlier chapter, life is moving rapidly, and many churches are not keeping up with the speed of these changes. Systematic, planned change should be the norm for every church just to keep up with the changes occurring in their mission fields (communities).

Unfortunately, change is frequently misunderstood. Some churches view change as an admission that they were doing something wrong. Others aren't sure when changes should be introduced, while other churches struggle with the types of changes that should occur. In this chapter we will try to answer some questions about change that are frequently asked by churches.

WHEN IS CHANGE NEEDED?

When Captain Michael Abrashoff assumed command of the *USS Benfold* in 1997, he found a dysfunctional ship manned by a crew that wanted to be anywhere but where they were. Although it was a new ship commissioned only a year earlier and equipped with the latest technology, it was not ready for duty due to the crew's attitude and the problems that attitude created. Captain Abrashoff made many changes during his stint as the ship's captain, but those changes began with the simple question he posed to every person on the ship, "Is there a better way to do what you do?"[2]

Such a question is a good starting point for church leaders to begin the process of identifying when changes need to be made. Changes should be made anytime we find a better way of doing what we do. However, there are two specific times when we need to implement changes: when things are going well in the church and when the church finds itself in trouble.

When things are going well

Surely I'm not serious when I suggest that small church leaders should be looking at implementing change when things are going well! Yes, I've heard the old adage "If it ain't broke, don't fix it," but that doesn't really apply anymore. That was a good saying back in the 1950s when things were made to last, but we live in a different time. What you have may not break, but it will quickly become obsolete in the twenty-first century. Our church programs and structures may not be broken, and they may have served us well for many years, but in many cases they are obsolete and impede the effectiveness of our ministries. These structures often become the filters through which any new idea must pass, and if the new idea doesn't fit in that structure, it is rejected.[3]

Human beings have a life cycle. We are born, we experience a time of growth, we settle into middle age, we get older, and we die. Churches experience a similar life cycle. They are born, they grow, they reach a plateau, and if nothing is done, they begin to decline until they finally die.[4] Aubrey Malphurs believes that up to 75 percent of all congregations founded before 1960 are either plateaued or declining.[5]

Just as a human being cannot stop the life cycle from continuing, neither can a church. However, a church can put off its eventual decline and death by starting a new life cycle, and the best time to do that is before the church reaches the plateau and certainly before it begins a period of decline.[6]

There are two important things to remember. Although we often speak of churches being on a plateau, churches really do not stay plateaued for very long. A church is either growing or declining. When a church stops growing, decline begins very quickly. The church may stay in the decline state for a very long time, even decades, but the decline will eventually lead to the death of the church.

The second thing a small church must remember is that once the church enters the decline state, it also enters a reactive mode. Survival becomes the primary goal, not growth. The few resources the church has will be used for survival, and these will quickly be depleted.[7]

Denial is the behavior I see used most often as a barrier. I see denial in congregations continuing to operate as if nothing has changed. Churches or congregations in denial look at downward patterns of membership and finance and talk about how it seems to be "bottoming out." Denial can be seen in the congregation that gradually eats up its reserves in deficit budgets year after year, with no thought to what comes next. Denial is a good word to describe churches who put off capital needs for future generations to face.[8]

> *Organizations need a new direction every two to three years.*[9]
> —Aubrey Malphurs

Small churches are resilient, but they will not be able to put off the inevitable forever. The president of LifeWay, Thom Rainer, predicts that 50,000 churches will close by 2010. Many of these churches were built and sustained by those born before 1946, but later generations find these churches do not meet their spiritual needs, and they have moved on to search for a church or group that will. When that Builder generation is gone, so will be the churches they built.[10] These churches have probably been in decline for years. Every effort to inject new life into them either failed or was rejected by those opposing change until the inevitable happens and their doors are closed.

When the church is in trouble

The signs of a church in trouble are obvious; but since denial is so strong in declining churches, let's list some of them anyway.

- Declining membership and attendance
- Declining finances
- New people soon leave
- Lack of new leaders
- Existing members unwilling to accept leadership positions
- Facility in poor repair and an unwillingness to spend money on it
- Aging membership
- Survival mentality
- Fond memories of the "good old days"
- Lots of blame toward those who are not committed to the church

At this point you may be ready to throw in the towel. You just checked off every item on this list as a description of your church. If you are the pastor, let me encourage you to not dust off your résumé just yet. In fact, that is probably one reason why your church is in this condition. For some strange reason, pastors accept a call to a small church thinking that people are going to be excited about their great, new ideas. They enjoy a brief honeymoon period, introduce their great, new ideas, and are shocked to discover that the congregation finds their ideas neither new nor great. As the opposition to their proposed changes intensifies, they begin the search for a new church that will better appreciate their great, new ideas. Their departure reinforces the congregation's belief that it was a good idea they didn't agree to the pastor's proposal since he or she wasn't going to stay around anyway. And the revolving door continues to trap the declining church in a state of despair and poor self-esteem, making it even more unlikely the members will accept any changes proposed by their next pastor.

If you are serious about wanting to introduce change into your church, you must be willing to make a long-term commitment to remain there as pastor. It can take several years for a pastor to earn the trust of a small church before he or she can even earn the right to suggest possible changes.[11] Once that right is earned, and a congregation approves of some significant change, expect it to take another three to five years to get that change implemented in the life of the congregation.[12]

Unfortunately, many small church leaders are not willing to wait that long to see needed changes occur in their churches. They abandon any hope of change occurring, and they depart their churches. In doing this, they leave the churches trapped in unhealthy patterns that will eventually lead to their demise.

WHY IS CHANGE SO DIFFICULT IN A SMALL CHURCH?

Part of the answer to this second frequently asked question is that a church is a living system, and one of the characteristics of a system is that it seeks balance. It prefers the status quo even when that status quo isn't healthy.

There are congregations who understand that things are not

what they should be, and they wish they were better. They dream of seeing their churches grow and enjoy healthy ministries in their communities. They speak of it often, especially when they are in the process of seeking new pastoral leadership. But they balk when new ideas are suggested that might lead to the fulfillment of those dreams. Why? Because they know the status quo; they do not know how the suggested changes might impact them. Even if they agree to the changes, it will take time to see the changes become part of their church culture. The system will seek balance and will oppose any effort to upset that balance.

In the status quo people know their roles. If changes occur, people no longer know what their roles might be, and even worse, some might not have roles in the new system. This can be very frightening to a person who sees his or her role in the church as the way he or she serves God.

Systems naturally and characteristically seek a balance, an equilibrium. If you push a system toward change, it naturally pushes back. If you push it harder, it pushes back harder in order to maintain its balance. If that is true of systems in general, it is particularly true of congregations, which maintain at least part of their identity through a history and tradition that many people feel must be preserved.[13]

I am familiar with a pastor of a large church who made an eleven-year commitment to the church when he began. As the church has needed to add staff, he has required all candidates to commit to staying at least five years if they accepted a position. The church has grown significantly, in part, because the congregation believes the pastor is not going to take off the first time things get a little difficult.

By now you are probably thinking that is fine for a leader of a large church with the resources and the desire to do significant ministry, but if I knew the situation you were in, I wouldn't be asking you to make a long-term commitment. I do know your situation because I pastored a church probably a lot like the one you serve. You can read part of the story in my first book, *The Tentmaking Pastor: The Joy of Bivocational Ministry.*[14] I stayed there for twenty years, and we saw a significant turnaround in the life and ministry of the church.

"Most desirable places were difficult until a previous pastor loved the church into greatness."[15] The most important question your congregation has for you is, "Pastor, do you love us?" Your congregation needs to know you love them enough to commit yourself to them and to the changes they need. Many small churches struggle today because the people have never received an affirmative answer to that question. Yes, we tell them we love them and that God has called us to serve them, but what do our actions tell them? Too often, we abandon them after the first or second difficulty and move on to where "God has called us" next.

What would you think of a spouse who left you every time things got a little difficult in your relationship? Despite assurances that he or she loves you, if that person who vowed to stay with you for better or worse abandoned you every couple of years, you would have serious doubts about his or her affection. You would also wonder what was so wrong with you that this person felt the need to leave you during times of difficulty instead of staying and resolving the problems. This is exactly how many of our small churches feel after being abandoned by their pastors every 12 to 24 months. Read this next statement very carefully: I doubt that any of us can truly understand how much pain may exist in the church we serve. That pain will only be healed when the congregation finally experiences the love of a pastor who is willing to commit his or her life to them.

> *Every assignment is holy ground because Jesus gave Himself for the people who live there.*[16]
> —H. B. London Jr.

Please, do not make any effort to introduce change in your church unless you are willing to commit yourself to that church for an extended period of time. If this church is just a step up the church ladder for you, don't do anything. Don't suggest any changes. Don't get the members' hopes up for something better. Be their chaplain, get your two years in, and move on. Don't add to their pain by getting their hopes up and leaving them.

If you are strongly committed to leading this church, change will still be difficult in a declining church, but it is possible. It will require much hard work, earnest prayer, and intentionality, but if you and the church are willing to do these things, transformation can occur.

WHAT CHANGES ARE NEEDED?

In the previous chapter we saw the importance of discerning a vision that will help the church understand where it is to go. Once this is done, the really hard work begins. How does the church get from where it is to where it is going? What stands in the way of the church achieving the vision it believes God has given it? Whatever stands between where you are today and where you believe God is leading you is what needs to be changed.

Some things must not be changed

It is important to understand what can be changed and what must not be changed. Perhaps the easiest way church leaders can tell the difference is by determining what things in the church are biblical and what things are cultural. Biblical teaching must not be sacrificed in the change process. Some churches are willing to forsake the sound theological teachings of Scripture, but in doing so they forfeit the right to proclaim themselves to be Christian organizations. Certain beliefs are essential to the Christian faith, and to forsake them is to forsake Christianity. Lists of essential beliefs may differ somewhat between churches, but at a minimum the list should include

- The inspiration of the Holy Scriptures
- The virgin birth of Jesus Christ
- The sinful nature of humanity
- The atoning sacrifice of Jesus Christ for the sins of all humanity
- The bodily resurrection of Jesus Christ
- The second coming of Jesus Christ

This list is not meant to be exhaustive because this is not the purpose of this book. You may disagree with some of the items on this list and would want to add more to it. That's all right, because my only purpose here is to point out that not everything within the church is open to change.

Biblical truth is not subject to change and cannot be ignored in an attempt to appeal to the unchurched. Although postmodernism has rejected the concept of absolute truth, it does not mean that such truth does

We believe that the church should be culturally relevant, while remaining doctrinally pure.[17]
—Bill Hybels

not exist. "The insistence on absolute truth is a massive and sharp stumbling block for postmoderns—given their absolute abhorrence of the absolute—but it cannot be softened or avoided if believers are to remain faithful to the truth of God."[18]

Jesus made a very dogmatic statement in John 14:6: "I am the way, the truth, and the life. No one comes to the Father except through Me." Is Jesus mistaken when He says this? Is He confused? Is He lying? Or is He speaking the truth? If we are to reject the first three possibilities, as I hope the reader will, it leaves only that He was speaking truth. Leonard Sweet writes: "Whenever I am interviewed, the question I'm almost always asked is this: 'Dr. Sweet, do you believe in absolute truth?' There is only one answer: 'I more than believe in it. I know Absolute Truth personally.' Absolute Truth is Jesus."[19] The church does not have to apologize for insisting that absolute truth exists and can be known when our Lord clearly states that such truth does exist and can be found in Him.

Some things can be changed

We've looked at some things that must not be changed, but what can we change to help a church become more missional? The general answer is we should change anything that keeps us from fulfilling our God-given vision as a church, but at the same time we need to be wise and discerning in what changes we try to make. We must avoid thinking we just need to make changes for the sake of making changes. We also want to be sure that the changes we make actually do help us move forward as a church.

Think systems, not programs

Small church leaders often contact me and tell me their problems, what they want to see happen, and then ask if I know of a new program they could use to achieve the desired results. Churches are always looking for a new program they can easily implement to solve their problems. Denominations and parachurch groups do a good job of developing new programs designed to address the problems of churches, but such programs do not bring about the transformation that churches need to provide ministry in the twenty-first century.

In chapter 2 we discussed the difference between transitional and transformational change. Introducing new programs is a type of transitional change. It is merely tweaking the church program a little. Types of programming change would include the switch to a new Sunday School curriculum, the formation of a new committee, or renovating the church property. Some churches have remodeled everything they own without really changing anything, and now they don't know what to do next.

This does not mean that programming changes are not important and/or needed in many churches. Worship services in many smaller churches could be improved simply by speeding up the music and keeping announcements to a minimum. Some churches have greeters who need a great deal of training before they should be allowed to continue in that position. From my experience of being in a different church almost every week, many smaller churches need to address hospitality issues so that guests feel welcomed and appreciated. Program changes can greatly benefit many churches, but these types of changes will not be enough to transform the church.

Transformational change occurs when the leaders begin to see the church as a system of interconnected parts. A programmatic view of the church looks at each component of the church and tries to fix those areas that appear to be broken. A systems view allows us to see the church

Your system is perfectly designed to produce the result you are getting.[20]

as an organism that works together, and any changes that are implemented will have an impact on the entire church system. This view also recognizes that an attempt to merely fix something that is broken is unlikely to have a long-term impact on the church. There must be a reason to focus on a particular area of brokenness.

Gil Rendle provides a helpful illustration to show the difference between a program view and a systems view of the church.[21] Imagine that you are in a church that is having financial problems. There is usually enough money to pay the monthly bills but little left over for ministry. In some situations this isn't even true. Expenses typically exceed giving, and the only way the church continues to operate is by dipping into its savings or endowment. Per capita giving has historically been low in the church. Any attempt to do something new is rejected because the church cannot afford it. Ministerial salaries are kept low, often resulting in a fairly rapid turnover of pastors.

Church leaders recognize they have a problem and immediately begin to think about how they might resolve it. They may ask their denomination if there is a new stewardship program they could use in their church. They may seek to reduce their budget and begin to cut expenses anywhere they can. Of course, one problem with reducing expenses is that the single largest expense in many smaller church budgets is pastor compensation, and reducing this is likely to make the turnover problem even worse. They might send out special appeals for funds to offset the declining offerings. Such a mechanical view tries to fix the problem but does nothing to understand why the problem exists. Rendle explains that "problems with or changes in finances and attendance at worship are often, or usually, not problems in and of themselves but reflect other issues in the life of the congregation."[22] A systems approach would seek to understand what those issues are.

A church looking at the problem of low finances from a systems perspective might find that

- Members of the congregation feel that the church has no sense of vision or purpose. People typically do not give abundantly to keep the utilities paid. They will give to a vision in which they believe and have ownership.
- There are conflict issues within the church that are impacting the finances. I have worked with conflicted churches in which people withheld their financial giving because they were in conflict with the pastor. In a small, family church a conflict between the leading families can also lead to reduced giving to the church.

- People feel they have been disenfranchised from the decision-making processes of the church. If their voice is not heard, perhaps their reduced financial giving will be. A good example of this is when people oppose a building program in the church, especially if it involves relocating the church facility to a new location. They reason that since the congregation ignored their input and voted to relocate the church, the congregation can pay for it without their help.

These are just a few examples of systemic issues that might result in decreased financial support in a church. No stewardship program, cost cutting, or special appeals will resolve these issues. Even if those stopgap methods resolve the immediate financial need, the issues still exist and will appear again and again until they are finally resolved. This is why you see unhealthy churches continue to have problems year after year and decade after decade. They have deep systemic issues that have never been addressed because church leaders keep looking for Band-Aid approaches to resolve the problems.

Systemic problems are the primary cause of unhealthy churches, and unhealthy churches will neither grow nor transform. All of their energies are spent fighting their problems, leaving little time or resources for ministry. For more information on healthy small churches and some diagnostic tools to help church leaders determine the health of their churches I refer the reader to my book *The Healthy Small Church: Diagnosis and Treatment for the Big Issues.*[23] Until the unhealthy issues are addressed, the church will remain stuck in a maintenance mode and will be unable to move forward.

Look for leverage points

Every small church has certain "untouchables" that the wise pastor will avoid when beginning the process of implementing change in the church. Trying to start the change process with these sacred cows will almost surely end badly and may shorten the tenure of the pastor. That does not mean these things do not need to be changed, but it does mean that they are not a good place to start. Look for those places that will give you the best return for your efforts with the least amount of conflict.

Church transformation can begin at any point, and at any place, in the system of congregational life. One begins where it is easiest to begin. That is, begin where permission is easiest to obtain. . . . Systemic change moves from celebration to celebration, rather than from victory to victory. The celebration of one successful experiment motivates the congregation to take greater subsequent risks.[24]

Malcolm Gladwell writes, "Starting epidemics requires concentrating resources on a few key areas."[25] The epidemic you want to begin in your church is transformation, and those few key areas are the leverage points that will enable that process to begin.

Every church will have different leverage points. These vary because of the personality of the church, the church's history, and because of the different visions and goals a church may have. As small church leaders determine those leverage points and begin to concentrate their efforts and resources to transform those areas, change can begin to happen in the church with minimal resistance.

Example of working with leverage points

Most small churches want to grow. I have worked with many churches as they sought new pastoral leadership, and they all claim they want a pastor who will help their church grow. Unfortunately, many of these churches are unwilling to pay the price to grow. A member of one small church called me one day to tell me the congregation had formed a growth committee in their church and wanted me to meet with that committee and explain how they could grow their church without making anyone upset. I told the caller I would save myself a trip and them a meeting because I could answer his question over the telephone, "You can't." They invited me to come anyway, and they have begun the process I discussed in an earlier chapter. This church is taking small, positive steps that should lead them into a new era of ministry.

> *Don't push growth; remove the factors limiting growth.*[26]
> —Peter M. Senge

Although someone will inevitably be upset when a church decides to take the steps needed to grow, there are some things a church can do to promote growth without upsetting too many people. One of the leverage points that exist in many small churches is hospitality. In my current ministry I visit a different church almost every week. While most churches make me feel welcome, I have visited more than a few, as I've implied earlier, that just did not know how to treat their guests. Most of these churches would call themselves friendly, but their guests are unlikely to agree. In some churches I have felt like an outsider that crashed a family get-together.

A few months ago my wife and I visited a small church for the first time. A Sunday School class of three senior adults had their class in the sanctuary, and nobody was allowed to enter until their class was over. Their class ended two minutes before the service was to start. We stood in the small foyer with about thirty other people. It was nearly impossible to jam one more person into that foyer. We stood there for twenty minutes waiting to enter the sanctuary, but not one person spoke a word to us. There was a lot of animated conversation all around us, but even though everyone knew this was our first visit to their church, no one spoke to us while we waited. When I relate this story to churches, I always ask two questions:

- What if I was someone who had recently moved into that community? How likely would it be that I would return to that church?
- A more important question: What if I was someone who was really struggling with life and searching for God? Would I have found Him there?

Every church should have at least one greeter at the door to welcome people and hand them a bulletin. It doesn't take much effort to smile, introduce oneself, and welcome them, but I have met some greeters who could not do that. I've also encountered some who didn't understand the importance of a breath mint, and that also makes an impression on a first-time guest!

When guests enter a church for the first time, they do not know where they should sit or where other people may sit. A good idea is to introduce guests to church members who are about the same age. The greeters can do this while they are welcoming them to the service. These church members can invite the guests to sit with them and begin to develop a relationship with them.

When I was growing up, it was common for visitors to be asked to stand, introduce themselves, and tell the church a little about themselves. People do not want to do that today, but some church-es still ask them to do so. Most guests find it embarrassing and do not want any kind of public recognition they are there. The last few years I pastored a small church, I would welcome our guests at the time we were taking up the offering. I never singled anyone out nor did I look at the guests as I was speaking. I simply welcomed our guests and told them the offering was the one part of the service that we asked that they not participate in. I would remind everyone that our members and regular attendees supported the ministry of our church and tell the guests that their presence with us that day was their gift to us. By doing this I welcomed the guests and took away one complaint unchurched people sometimes have about the church: "They are just interested in our money."

Another way we tried to make our guests feel comfortable was to put the page numbers from the pew Bibles in our bulletins for any Scripture reading. If they wanted to follow along, they did not have to worry about not being able to locate the passage; they could just turn to the page.

Another easy way to connect with people who might want to visit your church is to install an answering machine that gives the time of your services. George Barna released an update in 2004 that noted that nearly 20 percent of the 3,400 Protestant churches selected for their study did not answer the telephone in five separate attempts to call them during business hours. Neither a person nor an answering machine answered those calls.[27] This study did not break down the responses by church size, but probably the smaller churches would be even less likely to have someone answer the telephone during business hours. My experience has been that these churches are also less likely to have an answering machine, or if they do, they rarely provide the caller with the times of the worship services. Including this informa-tion on an answering machine is a very inexpensive way to make one more connection with your community.

None of these things are difficult; none should produce much conflict. Little, or no, cost is involved. It does, however, take some training and a change in people's mind-sets, but the returns could be great. These are good examples of leverage points that might exist in your church where you could begin the transformation process.

SIX

Introducing Change

Move slowly into change.[1]
—Kenneth O. Gangel

A church needed to build a new church building. They did what any good church would do—they turned the problem over to a committee. The committee did what it was supposed to do—discussed the problem for months. Finally, the committee presented to the church a proposal to build a new church building. After extended discussion, the church voted to build a new facility. They voted in favor of the following:

1. We will build a new church building.
2. We will build the new building on the same site as the old building.
3. We will build the new building using the materials out of the old building.
4. We will continue to meet in the old building until the new one is completed.

While I doubt the story is true, it does describe how many small churches approach change. Even when the needed change is apparent, the church will often balk at any proposed change and will make every effort to counter any attempt to implement the change. And they will often feel good about doing so![2]

YOUR CHURCH IS DIFFERENT

Perhaps what I've just said about churches and change isn't true about your church. Perhaps your congregation has determined that God is calling them to be a missional church and has spent time discerning God's vision for the future of their ministry. Maybe some of the needed changes have been identified. How are these changes now introduced into the congregation? The simple answer is v-e-r-y s-l-o-w-l-y.

Pastors sometimes believe a church when it tells them it is ready to change. This is especially true when a new pastor arrives at the church. He or she has believed everything the pastor search committee has told him or her. The committee insisted the church was seeking a pastor who could lead the church in exciting growth and new programs. When the candidate meets with other church leaders, they confirm that finding a pastor who can grow their church is their number one priority. The individual accepts the call to become the new pastor and quickly identifies several reasons the church isn't growing. Still believing everything the church said during the search period, the excited pastor begins to change the system and programming issues that are keeping the church from growing and is stunned to soon find out that he or she is asked to leave the church.

This would be a humorous story if it wasn't so true. LifeWay has conducted a study of terminated pastoral staff in the Southern Baptist Convention every year since 1996. Their study in 2005 found that more than 1,300 clergy were dismissed that year from their Southern Baptist churches. The top five reasons for the termination all include relational issues, including pastors trying to introduce change into the church. Perhaps the most interesting thing about their study is that the top five causes for clergy termination have been the same top five causes since they started doing the survey. The order of the five might change, but they remain the top five causes.[3]

What pastors and others in church leadership must remember is that they may have been focusing on transformation issues for some time. They have worked hard to understand the core values and bedrock beliefs of the church. They have met and prayed with one another to discern God's vision. It is all so clear to them because they have spent time identifying the things that need to change so the church can move forward. However, the rest of the congregation has not had that intense focus. The pastor and other leaders should not be surprised that there is so much resistance from the congregation when the proposed changes are first announced.

CREATE A CLIMATE FOR CHANGE

The first step in introducing change into a small church is to create a climate in which the congregation will support change.[4] This may well be the most difficult task for the person seeking to institute change, especially if the church is in a state of decline. The congregation is probably very change resistant, or they wouldn't be in the situation they

> *The first responsibility of a leader is to define reality.*[5]
> —Max DePree

are in. Innovation will be seen as a threat to their very survival, and it sends the message that what they are doing, and have been doing for many years, is wrong. It is not a message that will be well received.

Creating the right climate is important because of what is known about motivation. All real motivation comes from within an individual. As a small business owner I have had to let employees go because they refused to meet even the minimal expectations of our company. I talked to them, and I explained again and again the changes they would need to make if they continued to work for our company, but they simply refused to live up to the expectations. Even the threat of losing their jobs would not motivate them. To experience real change a person must have the inner motivation to want to change, and the most successful change agent will find a way to create a climate in which that self-motivation can occur.

CREATE A SENSE OF URGENCY

One of the important ways to create such a climate is to create a sense of urgency. John Kotter is a professor of leadership at the Harvard Business School. He believes the first step in creating a major change in an organization is to establish this sense of urgency.[6] In fact, the failure to create such urgency may be a primary reason that so many attempts to change fail. According to the book *Leading Congregational Change*, "Urgency is critical in the individual congregation. It creates a driving force that makes the organization willing to accept change and to challenge the conventional wisdom. It is no wonder that so many churches seem unwilling to change—they lack any sense of urgency."[8]

> *To be effective, a leader must also deliberately develop dissatisfaction.*[7]
> —Doug Murren

Complacency is common in smaller churches. Ask almost any small church member and he or she will tell you his or her congregation is warm and friendly. Most will profess a desire to reach new people and grow, but the fact is they are even more interested in the relationships that already exist within the church. Any effort to introduce change will be judged by the possible impact that change will have on their current relationships within the church.

Kotter cautions that we should "never underestimate the magnitude of the forces that reinforce complacency and that help maintain the status quo."[9] Again, that complacency in the smaller church is often due to the desire to keep the relational nature of the church intact. These churches are not called family churches without reason. Unless the change agent can first create a sense of urgency regarding the need for the proposed change, it will almost always fail.

WAYS TO CREATE A SENSE OF URGENCY

It is often helpful to have someone from outside the church assist in creating the dissatisfaction needed to gain a sense of urgency. A denominational minister or a consultant might more effectively speak about the gap that exists between what is and what should be in the church. Certainly, they can talk about what other churches of similar size are doing to help lift the vision of the congregation. They can lead a discussion about what a missional church could look like and how a particular church could move into that model.

Our regional office currently offers a process called Church Alive Next Generation, which assists a congregation in seeking God's vision for their church. In larger churches we normally work with the leadership teams in the church, but in smaller churches we work with the entire congregation. Once the leadership team or congregation discerns the direction they believe God is leading them, we then help resource them so they can achieve that vision. The pastor participates with the church and is not involved in leading the process. This allows the church to hear another voice advocating for change in its ministry.

Take some key leaders who are more open to change to visit other churches with effective ministries. Most people in leadership are willing to talk to others about how their ministries have evolved over time. You are not looking for programs that you can take back to your church to duplicate, but you are looking for a mind-set that will help your congregation be more open to some new things God might want to do in their lives. Encourage these leaders to discuss what they saw in the churches you visited. Give them time in the worship services and other church gatherings to talk about what they learned from talking to the leaders of the other churches. Let their excitement rub off on rest of the congregation.

Allow some things to fail. One Sunday morning I announced to the church that I was no longer going to go behind people and do the work they didn't do. Like many churches, we had some people who wanted certain positions in the church but were not willing to do the work. Someone, often I, would cover for them to ensure that their responsibilities were done. I simply told the church that if someone accepted a responsibility, and it wasn't done, it would remain undone. Furthermore, if anyone came to ask why something had not been done, I would direct that person to ask the individual responsible. A few things failed to get done after that, and people saw that I was serious. Very quickly the problem resolved itself, but my statement and actions pointed out that a change was necessary if the church was going to function effectively.

Constantly remind the congregation of the ministry opportunities that exist in the community. Talk about them in sermons, in the newsletter, and in every communication tool you have. Lift up the needs in the community and invite the congregation to consider how they might meet those needs. Remind them of what might happen if those needs are not met. Because no one rejects his or her own ideas, allow them to come up with solutions to the needs you identify. Coaching skills are important for this, and persons committed to introducing change need to learn some of these skills.

Make those needs personal. In many small churches the pastor would only need to point out the absence of young people, including those who are children of the church members. Remind them it was because of the efforts and sacrifices of the former members of the church that the church is here for them today. Then ask what will be the fate of their children and grandchildren if the church doesn't develop new ministries to appeal to these young people and meet their needs. This makes the proposed change personal.

> *The key to transformation is not the mind but the will.*[10]
> —Thomas Bandy

People can be rather uncaring about "people in our community," but when you put faces and names on those people, and those faces and names are related to members of the congregation, those needs take on a whole different meaning.

I was recently in a church that I had not visited in a couple of years. When I was there the previous time, the congregation had just introduced a praise band to their worship service. I know this congregation. They are very traditional, blue-collar people living in a rural community. Their new praise band played music that bordered on heavy metal music and seemed to be out of place in this church. Now on this latest visit I noticed the band's music was not any quieter, but some major changes had taken place. There were noticeably more younger people in the sanctuary. Older members were singing along and moving to the beat of the music, and the younger people were singing to the hymns when they were played. There was a great worshipful atmosphere in the church. Another even more significant change had also occurred. I was told that every member of the band had recently invited Jesus Christ into their lives and been baptized. In addition, a number of their parents and grandparents had begun attending the church, and some of them had also recently become Christians. The kingdom of God has grown because this small church was willing to allow changes in its worship experience.

Speak openly and honestly about the problems in the church and the bleak future the church has if things continue as they are. Many church members and leaders like to speak only "happy talk." Don't let them. Point out the realities that face the church, but remember that the prophet is not always the most appreciated person in a community.

Even a brief study in the Old Testament reveals that people usually don't like the message of a prophet. Things haven't changed in the twenty-first century. Many people don't want to hear the truth even if they know it is the truth. The challenge for the modern prophet is to create a sense of urgency without getting stoned, or fired. The minute you suggest that some change is needed, you are implying that the church is not functioning properly. People will begin to get very uncomfortable.

You're trying to turn up the heat, which is guaranteed to make people uncomfortable, and they are going to pressure you to turn the heat down. The challenge for the leader is to keep the heat high enough to motivate the congregation but not so high that they become paralyzed. This balancing act requires the leader to constantly take the temperature of the group so he or she knows whether to turn the heat up or let things cool down a little.[11] However, measuring the temperature of the congregation is too important for a single leader to do alone. Ron Crandall insists that

> timing and patience are much more important in small congregations than in large ones, and listening to the pulse of the congregation ought to be the job of many and not just the one. It is a mistake to go it alone, trusting only one's own intuitions without checking with several honest friends in the church, including some who might disagree.[12]

TURNING DOWN THE HEAT

How can a leader cool things down a little? The simplest way is by backing off for a time. Feeding the congregation a steady diet of problems and predictions of dire consequences won't only turn up the heat too much; it will also get the leader in hot water! Remember the earlier admonition of taking the long view. The church did not get into its current difficulties overnight, and they won't resolve them overnight. The change you are proposing probably doesn't need to be accomplished today. Pointing out the challenges facing the church will crank up the heat, and backing off for a while to allow the congregation to absorb your suggestions and thoughts will let them cool back down. By regularly checking with the congregation you'll know whether it's time to turn the heat back up or to allow a little more cooling time. This balancing act is difficult but necessary if the leader wants to be there to see the change enacted.

Another way of cooling things down a little is to show only the smaller changes that need to be made. Most changes consist of several steps, and to reveal the entire change that needs to occur is likely to overwhelm some small churches. It just seems too large and impossible, but if only the first steps of the change are presented, much of that fear can be eliminated. Creating urgency while controlling the temperature can help overcome the resistance and conflict likely to occur when the proposed change is suggested.

CONFLICT IS INEVITABLE

Lyle Schaller assures us that "the only safe assumption is the immediate, natural, and normal response of every individual will be to reject any and all proposals for change in favor of perpetuating the status quo."[13] Any study of the Bible and church history will demonstrate that change does not happen without conflict. Unfortunately, conflict is not always civil. God's people have proven they can be violent and destructive. I know of conflict in one church that included threats to burn down the parsonage. Fortunately, this did not happen.

Although most conflict is unlikely to turn so violent, it can still be damaging to the church and to the community. It can result in pastors being fired, people leaving the church, and even church splits. At the very least it will create hard feelings and distrust that can take years to overcome. A hidden result of church conflict is often the negative impact it has on the church's ability to minister to the community. Unchurched people can often remember church fights that occurred years earlier, and they use these conflicts as their excuse to not become involved with a church.

> *Assume that everyone but you will absolutely hate your plan, at least initially.*[14]
>
> —Hans Finzel

Why does such conflict occur whenever significant change is proposed to a church? One reason is that many people simply do not like change. Herb Miller explains:

A national study by *American Demographics* magazine reported that 47 percent of Americans are highly resistant to change. Another 17 percent of Americans are peace lovers. They do not actively resist change, but they prefer that no one rock the boat. Who do the 17 percent side with when someone suggests a change? The vocal 47 percent that strongly resist change, of course. Result: Expect 64 percent of governing-board members and church staff to vote against a new idea the first time they hear it.[15]

A friend of mine visited a church one Sunday and was asked to move twice before the service started. In each case he was informed he was sitting in someone's seat, although there was nothing in the seat to indicate someone had previously claimed it. Of course, each person had claimed it through years of sitting in the same pew year after year. I guess you could call it squatter's rights.

We are creatures of habit, especially in smaller churches. The same people hold the same offices year after year. We sit in the same pews week after week. Everyone knows his or her role in the small church. It provides us with a sense of security and stability that we cannot experience

"Change management" often becomes "pain management."[16]
—Jeff Woods

in any other area of our lives. Everything else in our lives is changing so dramatically that we often feel lost in the chaos. But on Sunday mornings we can go to our normal seats, assume our normal responsibilities, and enjoy our usual worship service.

The moment someone mentions change we become fearful because, as mentioned earlier, change means that our roles might change. We aren't even sure there will be a role for us in this new environment that is being proposed, and the stability we have felt in the church for years is threatened. The perceived loss of identity and stability causes people to resist the change that is causing this loss. It is not the change people resist; it is the perceived loss they believe the change is going to cause them that they resist.[17]

Some people will resist change because it is a threat to their kingdom. Thomas Bandy estimates that about 20 percent of a congregation could be classified as "controllers" and believes that number could be even higher in a declining church.[18] Controllers believe that the church exists to meet their personal and family needs. They work hard to control the finances, the decisions, and the mission of the church. Anytime they feel their control is slipping, they will threaten to leave or withhold their financial giving, and the small church will often give in to their threats. After all, this is a family church, and the fear of losing a family member is too overwhelming to consider. Naturally, controllers will reject any change that appears to threaten their own private kingdom created within the church.

Bandy also talks about the cult of harmony that exists in many of our churches today.[19] These churches prefer harmony to truth. They prefer harmony to mission. Rather than standing up to the controllers and confronting them with the mission God has given the church, these churches give in to the controllers' childish demands and threats and sacrifice the mission. As a result, these churches remain stuck in unhealthy habits and practices, while the community around them remains untouched by God.

Any time significant change is introduced into a church, there is the possibility that you will lose some people. The fact is that you are already losing people. If you introduce the change, you may lose those who oppose the change. If you abandon the change, you will lose the potential people the church could have reached and those who were in favor of the change. As a leader in the church, you get to choose who you will lose and who you will keep.

A few years ago I worked with a small church that was embroiled in great conflict. The church had very nice facilities and was in an excellent location in the community. This church had great potential that had never been realized. Many people visited this church each year, but few stayed. Of those who did join the church, many soon left because of the constant turmoil. The leadership board mentioned that the new members were often the best financial supporters of the church and the most promising leaders. Because they were leaving, the church was having financial problems and difficulty in finding enough people for the various positions in the church. All the turmoil came from a small handful of controllers that no one wanted to confront. I asked the leadership who they preferred to keep in the church: the controllers or the people they kept running off. They wanted to keep the new people, but they were unwilling to confront the controllers. In that case, I assured them they would continue to have the same problems that had affected the church for years.

The leadership board decided to act. Within a few weeks one of the problem families took some steps that again caused some newer members to leave the church. The board called this family in for a meeting and informed them that their behavior would no longer be tolerated. The family left. The church soon called a new pastor who, within three months after arriving, confronted another controller in the church who also decided to leave. Suddenly, the church began to grow and a new spirit was soon felt in the church. Today, this church has doubled in attendance since my initial visit, and their finances have improved threefold.

As a leader in your church you must decide whether you want to keep the controllers or reach new people for the kingdom of God. Bandy asks the question in powerful terms:

All you need to ask is: "Do you love controllers more than your own children, parents, neighbors, and work associates?" Is it more important to keep controlling clergy, matriarchs, patriarchs, wealthy trustees, or domineering institutional managers, rather than welcome your own teenagers, parents, and immediate loved ones into the community of faith? The choice may be as profound as "Christ or Institution," but for most people it is as simple as "Controller or my teenager." If one must go so the other can belong, what will be your preference?[20]

Sometimes the conflict will arise because people simply do not understand the proposed change or the need for it. That is why we addressed communication in chapter 3. Much conflict can be avoided in a change process if the change was carefully explained through effective communication.

RAISE THE EXPECTATIONS

What are the current expectations of your congregation? If it is like most smaller churches, these expectations normally include maintaining the church in its current form. The congregation expects the pastor to be available to minister to the needs of the congregation. They expect the times and format of the worship service to be convenient and appropriate to their needs. They expect that all bills will be paid on time and that no decision will be made impacting the life of the church without the opportunity to approve it before its implementation. Perhaps their primary expectation is that the church doors will be open for as long as they live. The problem with these expectations is that they are focused on satisfying the needs of the current membership. The congregation has little, or no, real expectation that they will have any genuine impact on the community they have been called to serve.

As noted in chapter 1, this is not the case with missional churches. Milfred Minatrea tells us that

missional churches *expect* to transform the world through involvement and ministry. Beginning with their own city, they extend their focus to their state, their nation, and the ends of the earth. They believe the Gospel is still the power of God to transform all who believe. [Emphasis added][21]

There is a big difference between the expectation that the church will meet the needs of the congregation and the expectation that it will transform its world. One of the keys to introducing change into the church is to raise the expectations of the congregation.

> *The blueprint for becoming a breakout church requires becoming a high-expectation church.*[22]
> —Thom Rainer

Coaches and business leaders have learned that people tend to live up to the expectations others have of them. If a team does not expect to win a game, it is very unlikely that they will. If a player loses confidence and does not believe he or she will make the shot, the player normally won't and is unlikely to even take the shot. If a congregation does not believe that their efforts will make any real difference in the lives of other people, they are unlikely to minister to other people. They will be satisfied to show up on Sunday and be spiritual consumers.

Our congregations need to understand that real ministry occurs outside the walls of the church each week as God's people move about the workplace, the marketplace, and in our communities. We gather together on Sunday to worship and celebrate all God has done for us and to be instructed and equipped for the ministry opportunities that will be around us the remainder of the week. Merely showing up on Sunday to sing a few songs and hear a sermon isn't what is expected of God's people. We are to be ambassadors of Jesus Christ, salt and light to a hurting world, and the instruments through which God can touch the lives of other people, enabling them to experience the same transformation that occurred within us when He touched our lives.

Our congregations need to be challenged to really believe that this is the way they should function and to expect God to use them to bring such transformation to those people they encounter each day. Missional churches thrive in such expectations.

REFUSE TO GIVE UP

Introducing change to a small church requires a great deal of wisdom and patience. As we have seen, most congregations will not readily embrace change the first time it is presented. Change agents within the church will normally have to calm the fears of many people and patiently answer the same questions over and over again. Conflict management and resolution skills are a necessity. Some people will threaten to leave the church, and some are likely to do so. These are always painful times because no real spiritual leader wants to see people walk away from the church, especially if they have invested much of their lives in it. Only my wife knows the amount of pain I experienced every time a member of our church left because he or she got upset over something we were doing. In some cases, the church was probably better off without that person's negativity, but that did not lessen the pain I felt.

Frankly, it would be easier to simply minister the way the church desires and the way many of us have been taught by our seminaries. Such maintenance ministry seldom rocks the boat and will probably not offend too many people. However, it is unlikely you would have read this far if you were not committed to leading your church through the changes necessary to a more missional ministry. The best advice I can give you at this point is to refuse to give up. George Barna writes with great conviction, "Intentional and strategic change—especially on a major scale—occurs because it has been tirelessly pushed through by believers with blinders."[23]

This does not mean that change agents force change upon a church. Such efforts are almost always doomed to fail and are likely to result in persons being removed from leadership positions. However, if a person takes the long view and continues to promote change, such change is possible even in the most resistant church. Small steps are usually the best, and you should always begin where there is greatest possibility of success. Set short-term goals that can be achieved within six to eighteen months, and people are more likely to continue on the transformation journey.[24]

Jill Hudson asks the defining question for our churches: "The question before us is, Will the church in the postmodern world become a museum or a movement? Will we become, like the apostolic church, a missional community, or will we remain inwardly focused, continuing to do the same things and working harder at it, but hoping for a different outcome?"[25] If you are a leader in your church and committed to being on mission with God in your community, you must refuse to give up the effort to lead the changes that may be required to transform your church into a missional congregation.

WHAT DOES A
missional church
look like?

It is always helpful to have an image of the destination in your mind before starting a journey. In this section we want to create an image of what a missional church looks like. Having said that, we must quickly add that no two missional churches will look exactly alike. There is no cookie-cutter approach to being a missional church. It is not a one-size-fits-all. But there are some similarities found in missional churches, and these are what we will examine in this section.

SEVEN

Missional Churches Understand Their Culture

> *To be faithful to its calling, the church must be contextual; that is, it must be culturally relevant within a specific setting.*[1]
> —Craig Van Gelder

My definition of a missional church is much simpler than the definition that many others use. A missional church is a church that is on mission with God. Everything else is contextual. A missional church in West Virginia is likely to look much different from a missional church in Seattle. The Thousand Hills Cowboy Church in Texas will be quite different from the Edgeworth Church near Boston. However, they will have one major similarity. Each understands the culture of the community they are trying to reach, and they are committed to working within that culture to advance the kingdom of God.

Many churches do not understand the culture in which they currently exist. They do not understand that Ozzie and Harriet have not been on television since 1966. They have been replaced by Ozzy Osbourne and his family. Bart Simpson has replaced Beaver Cleaver, and MTV doesn't look anything like *American Bandstand* with Dick Clark. We might prefer to be able to minister in simpler times, but that is not an option. We have to minister to the present culture where we are, and in order to do that we must understand that culture and enter into it.

A WARNING

This does not mean that we are to become one with the culture. I believe that some churches have made the mistake of wanting to enter into our modern-day culture so badly that they have compromised their values in an effort to be in step with the times. A pastor in Detroit upset some of his congregation and other area churches with a sermon series on sex. On the first Sunday in Lent he preached a sermon titled "The Greatest Sex You'll Ever Have." The church's Web site promoted the series with a video that started with two pairs of feet sticking out of the covers and shoes lying next to clothing.[2]

Does the missional church need to address issues of sexuality? Absolutely. The Bible has much to say about human sexuality, and the church does people a disservice if it ignores this important aspect of our lives. Pastors and other church leaders need to address human sexuality frankly and honestly, but never crudely. Did this sermon series and the promotional video cross the line in good taste? That is a decision that the congregation will have to make, but each of us needs to be aware that there is a fine line we must not cross in order to connect to our culture. John MacArthur sounds a warning that the church needs to hear.

Worldly preachers seem to go out of their way to put their carnal expertise on display—even in their sermons. In the name of connecting with "the culture" they want their people to know they have seen all the latest programs on MTV; familiarized themselves with all the key themes of "South Park"; learned the lyrics to countless tracks of gangsta rap and heavy metal music; and watched who-knows-how-many R-rated movies. . . . They've adopted both the style and the language of the world—including lavish use of language that used to be deemed inappropriate in polite society, much less in the pulpit. They want to fit right in with the world, and they seem to be making themselves quite comfortable there.[3]

I must admit that I am also often troubled by the profanity I hear from Christians and Christian leaders. Perhaps I am oversensitive because when I came out of the Navy, I had a very foul mouth. When I gave my life to the Lord a few years later, I felt that my language needed to change, but it appears that many believers do not feel that way today. Vulgarity and crudity do not assist a believer in Jesus Christ toward sanctification and holiness.

> *And do not become conformed to this world, but be transformed by the renewing of your mind, that you may prove what is that good and acceptable and perfect will of God.*
>
> —Rom. 12:2

We are in this world, but we are not to be of the world (John 17:16). We need to understand our society and engage it, but we must not become so closely identified with society that there is no discernable difference between Christians and unbelievers. We are to be the salt of the earth to help people thirst for Christ and to preserve this world in which we live. Our lives are to reflect the light of Jesus Christ so others will be drawn to Him. None of this can happen if we allow the world to shape our language and behavior.

Churches that become one with the culture really misunderstand what it means to be a missional church. Mennonite minister Lois Barrett writes:

> Key images of God's alternative community, the missional church, are found in the Gospels' descriptions of the people of God as "the salt of the earth," a "light of the world," and a "city set on a hill." These images suggest that mission is not just what the church *does;* it is what the church *is.* Saltiness is not an action; it is the very character of salt. Similarly, light or a city set on a hill need not do anything in order to be seen. . . . Who the community is and how it lives points to God and is an invitation to join the community in praising God.[4]

The missional church must understand the culture in which it is doing ministry; it must enter into that culture and find ways to present the gospel of Jesus Christ that will speak to the needs of the culture, but it must not become one with the culture. The church will have failed if those outside the church cannot tell where the culture ends and the church begins. Such churches might win a hearing from those outside the church, but it is unlikely those who are attracted to such churches will ever grow as disciples of Jesus Christ.

STUDYING THE CULTURE

In the first section of this book I encouraged your church to identify the target audience God has given your church to reach. Each audience will have its own traits, and each church will have to identify those characteristics if it wants to successfully reach its target group. A missionary does not normally go immediately to his or her mission field when commissioned. There is a time of preparation as the missionary must learn the language, customs, dress, and culture of the area where he or she will serve. A missional church must also spend time understanding the community it wishes to reach.

There is no cultureless gospel. Jesus himself preached, taught, and healed within a specific cultural context. Nor is it the case that the gospel can be reduced to a set of cultureless principles. The message of the reign of God, the gospel, is always communicated with the thought constructs and practices within the cultural setting of the church in a specific time and place.[5]

Demographic information is available that can help a church begin this study, but such information is not enough. Some churches may decide God is calling them to reach the growing Hispanic population that is found in many communities, but they struggle, and often fail, when they try. If God was calling them to reach this culture, why were they not more successful in their efforts? Perhaps they did not understand that there are differences in Hispanics from different parts of the world, and these differences must be respected to enjoy a successful ministry with people from that culture. Many churches seek a Spanish-speaking pastor to lead these new churches, not realizing that a Spanish-speaking pastor may not be attractive to second-generation Hispanics who prefer speaking English. There is not one Hispanic culture; there are many Hispanic cultures. There is not one African-American culture; there are many African-American cultures just as there are many different cultures found among Caucasians and every other people group.

Some smaller churches seem to be unaware that the culture around their church is changing. A number of years ago many communities saw their neighborhoods changing. People left the inner cities for the suburbs. Others left their farms and moved into more populated communities seeking better job opportunities. At the same time, some people moved from the city into the country seeking a quieter life. Immigrants began moving into many communities throughout North America. Some communities have changed dramatically, and churches in many of those communities continue doing church as they have for generations, and they cannot understand why they continue to see their church's impact on the community lessen with each passing year. A missional church is reaching out to the people who live in their communities today, not those who lived there two or three decades ago. A church must continue to study its surrounding culture if it wants to impact that community.

STUDYING THE GENERATIONAL DIFFERENCES

Much has been written lately about the differences between the various generations existing in North America. The builders are those who were born between 1925 and 1946. They survived two world wars and a great depression. They are known for their hard work, frugality, and patriotism. They built the infrastructure that has helped make the economy of this nation so strong. Their strong faith and institutional loyalty also helped build our churches and denominations. Builders have traditionally provided the leadership and have been willing to serve in the various volunteer positions that are needed in our churches. Much of the financial support of our existing churches comes from this generation, and there is already concern about how the church will do financially as this generation continues to grow smaller in size.

No generation has attracted more interest than the baby boomers who were born between 1946 and 1964. This is currently the largest segment of our population. Although they enjoyed affluence and educational opportunities not known by previous generations, they were a rebellious generation who became known as the hippie generation. Sex, drugs, and rock and roll became a mantra among many of this group. However, this

> *American Christianity is dominated by our parents' generation. And we boomers, despite our desire to return to a real spiritual experience, are unable to relate to a church culture dominated by our parents.*[6]
> —Doug Murren

generation was also deeply involved in ending racial segregation and creating new opportunities for women as well as minorities. Baby boomers want to be active even as they enter into their retirement years, and a church that is serious about reaching segments of this culture must provide opportunities for them to be involved in the life of the church.

Busters were born between 1965 and 1976. This generation is less likely to attend church than any other present generation. They are almost the forgotten generation. Many in this generation have struggled with employment and financial stability. A significant percentage comes from divorced families, which may account for the emphasis many pastors from this generation place on ministering to families and children.[7] Churches that effectively reach this generation will use drama, movies, music, and stories to share the story of Jesus Christ.

Millennials, or bridgers, were born between 1977 and 1994. They comprise the second largest generation in North America. Although it is a very spiritual generation, bridgers do not necessarily believe that their spiritual needs can be met through the church. Strongly influenced by postmodernism, many in this generation reject any message that claims to contain absolute truth. For many the only absolute truth is that there is no absolute truth. This is

Many of the bridgers will bring to church their baggage of guilt and low self-esteem. The growing churches of the twenty-first century will be those that proclaim that sin can be forgiven and low self-esteem can be transformed into high self-esteem through Christ.[8]
—Thom Rainer

another generation strongly impacted by broken families.

There is not time or space in this book for a thorough study of the various generations. I only share these brief descriptions to point out some of the major differences existing between the generations and to illustrate how important it will be to focus the majority of your efforts and resources on reaching out to a specific segment of society. Trying to be all things to all people as a missional church is as much a certain recipe for disaster as is trying to reach a specific group without fully understanding that group.

Many of our churches have all four generations currently attending the services and this often creates problems. How does a small church provide a meaningful worship experience for different generations who have very different needs, different music preferences, and different value systems? How does a pastor prepare a message that will speak to those differences? This is a challenge that will not get easier over time, and it is something that our churches need to openly address. Again, I would start with the question of who are we here for and let the discussion flow as the church seeks an answer. As much as we may want to say that we are here to reach everyone, it is going to be increasingly more difficult to do that as the generation gaps continue to widen.

Often, when a discussion of this type begins, it is assumed that the church needs to ignore the needs of the older generations in order to reach younger people. A missional church identifies the audience God is leading it to reach, and it is a mistake to always assume that means the church must gear itself to younger people. A missional church can target reaching the builder generation just the same as it might target reaching the millennials. Not every builder is a believer in Jesus Christ, and not every builder is involved in a church. There continues to be a mission field for builders in America, and if your church consists primarily of builders, this might be the target your church could most effectively reach.

Baby boomers are also growing older, and the oldest of us are nearing retirement age. Many of us enjoy more traditional worship services, and there will continue to be a need for those types of services. Many baby boomers have still not been reached with the gospel, and intentional ministries to do so are greatly needed. Being a missional church is not about merely removing the organ and bringing in a rock band and having the pastor preach without a suit and tie. A missional church is a church that is on mission with God regardless of what that mission is. A church can remain a very traditional church in many ways and still be missional if it understands its current God-given vision and is seeking to fulfill that vision.

STUDYING THE NEEDS OF THE COMMUNITY

I have always been impressed with how Jesus ministered to the specific needs of the people He encountered. Some Christian leaders continue to reject the importance of needs-based preaching and needs-based ministry, but Jesus is always seen in Scripture ministering to the needs of the people. By ministering to their physical needs He was able to minister to their spiritual needs as well. This seems to be a good model for a missional church to follow.

What needs exist in your community and especially in the target group your church seeks to reach? Does that target group need someone to help them learn English? Is there a need for day care for their children? Today, a better question might be, Is there a need for day care for aging parents so their children who care for them can go to work without worrying about them all day? If your community has legalized gambling, there may be a need for a ministry to people who are addicted to gambling. Is there a need for a ministry to people who have been divorced? What about a ministry for people who have recently lost their spouses? Several years ago our church found that there were several new widows in our community, and we began a ministry to bring them together to share with one another. It didn't last a real long time, but the women all said that it was helpful as they transitioned to being single again after losing their husbands.

In chapter 4 I mentioned the bivocational pastor who asked me about her idea of reaching out to people in the community who had been hurt in the past by a church. She knew of a few people in their community that were not interested in attending church because they had been deeply hurt by a church in the past. I assured her there were probably more than a few people in that situation in every community and that such a ministry could have a great impact in people's lives.

How does a church identify these needs in their communities? By being involved in the community and asking questions. Maintenance churches have the attitude that their doors are open for anyone who wants to enter. Missional churches are out in their communities meeting people and learning about the needs that exist there. They leave the comfort of their four walls and their cozy Christian fellowships and enter the world they seek to take for Christ.

Although I am not a big fan of Whoopi Goldberg, I do enjoy watching *Sister Act*. In the movie Goldberg is a nightclub singer who has to hide from the mob by pretending to be a nun. She soon is asked to lead the church's choir, which is dreadful. Not only does she change the music the choir sings to a much more contemporary style, but she also leads the nuns out of the confines of their church into a very rough community with many needs. The mother superior opposes both the change in music and the involvement of the nuns in the community. She insists the community is much too dangerous for the nuns. Her objections are ignored, and soon the dying church is filled each Sunday by people wanting to know more about these folks who are engaged in making their community better, as well as wanting to hear the upbeat music of the choir.

This is exactly what the missional church has to do. Yes, the world in which we live is a dangerous place with many people who do not believe as we do. But we will not engage them from within the comfort and security of those walled fortresses we call churches. We will not know who they are or what needs they have if we merely gather together in our holy huddle each week and then hurry home so we can avoid the unchurched people who live within our communities. Missional churches will be in their communities identifying the hurts and needs of the people for whom Jesus died and seeking ways to minister to those hurts and needs.

The challenge for small churches is that they will identify many more needs than they can possibly meet. How can the church discover which needs they should minister to and which ones they should ignore and trust God to minister to through another church? One tool that can be used is a SWOT analysis, which is discussed in the Appendix.

STUDYING THE COMMON TRAITS OF OUR TWENTY-FIRST-CENTURY SOCIETY

This chapter has looked at three areas a church needs to study in its community, but there are also some common traits existing in society today that the missional church will need to understand and address. These include loneliness, incivility, and fear.

Loneliness

Many, if not most, of the homes in the rural community where I grew up had large front porches that invited neighbors to stop and visit. I can remember many evenings when family, friends, and neighbors would visit with my parents sitting on that front porch chatting about the events of the day. Sometimes we would break out the old hand-crank ice cream maker and make some delicious homemade ice cream. One farm we owned had a cistern that had the coolest, freshest water in the area. We kept an old metal cup on the pump handle, and sometimes neighbors would stop their work in nearby fields to get a cup of water out of the cistern. We attended the local Baptist church in every community in which we lived, were involved in the PTA, shopped at the local grocery stores, and became a part of the community. We knew our neighbors, and if anyone needed help, they knew they could count on the community to assist.

Today, most of us do not know many of our neighbors. We don't build houses with big front porches anymore. Instead, we build houses with big back decks and surround those with privacy fences. We come home from work, use our remote to open the garage door, pull our car into the garage so no one will know whether we are home, and go sit on the back deck surrounded by the privacy fence. We use caller ID to screen our calls. And we are so lonely.

I was fortunate to have been born into a culture that valued community, but that is not the culture that exists today. Today's culture is one of individualism. Randy Frazee explains this means that "when we gather in a room, we gather as a group of individuals who are concerned about our individual wants and needs, not as a community united around some common characteristics."[9] The question on people's minds today is, "What's in it for me?" By the way, that's the same question often asked in the maintenance church. If some proposal or idea doesn't benefit me or my family, I'm not going to support it. I might not fight it, but I won't be involved.

Robert Putnam has written that between 1985 and 1994 active involvement in community organizations in America fell by 45 percent.[10] In the mid-1970s the average American entertained friends in their homes fourteen to fifteen times a year, but by the late 1990s that number had fallen to eight times per year, another 45 percent decline.[11] Based upon a study conducted by the American Bowling Congress, Putnam reported that between 1980 and 1993 the number of bowlers in America increased by 10 percent, but league bowling declined by more than 40 percent.[12] In fact, most group sports have seen a decline in recent years, while individual activities such as walking and treadmills have increased. We are increasingly becoming a society that is isolating ourselves from others in our community; and based upon a report from George Gallup Jr., we are among the loneliest people in the world.[13]

The odd thing is that we want to be connected to others. Starbucks has created a structure that has enabled them to experience great growth. They call this structure the "Five Ways of Being," which includes "Be Welcoming." They define Be Welcoming

We're not in the coffee business serving people. We're in the people business serving coffee.[15]

—Howard Schultz

as "offering everyone a sense of belonging."[14] They do this by learning their regular customers' names, their favorite drinks, and providing them a warm and inviting "Third Place" for their lives. Starbucks stresses that "Everything Matters" when it comes to serving their customers.

Missional churches look for ways to tap into this desire people have for community. Because they are involved in their neighborhoods, they are able to build authentic relationships with people. The key word here is "authentic." A missional church seeks to build real relationships with people because they love and respect all those who have been created in the image of God. They build relationships because they genuinely care for people, not because they are seeking another notch on their evangelistic program.

That authenticity continues when people visit the church. Like Starbucks, they offer everyone a sense of belonging. They avoid making people feel uncomfortable by speaking churchese and using language that seems to pit "us" against "them." People are made to feel that they are really welcome there.

What makes congregations so appealing in our culture is that, in most places, they are the closest thing to an intimate community that is available to people—and being part of a community is a powerful basic human need.[16]

—Israel Galindo

Smaller churches are naturally relational and should find it easy to offer a sense of community to the people in its communities. However, this again depends on whether the smaller church is focused on maintenance or mission. A maintenance church will be cautious of new people because new people might upset the balance of power in the church. Maintenance churches offer a facade of friendliness and community, but unchurched people can usually see through that facade rather easily. I have been in a number of churches filled with smiling people who welcomed me and invited me back, but at the same time I felt that I was an unwelcome guest at a family get-together. Missional churches are excited to have more people become a part of their family.

Incivility

We live in a mean-spirited world. As I write this, CBS and MSNBC announced they had fired Don Imus for remarks he made about the Rutgers' women's basketball team. Michael Richards recently went on a rampage during a standup comedy routine and used racist language against two men who made him angry during his performance. Rosie O'Donnell regularly makes negative comments about Christians and conservatives, and Christians and conservatives often say some harsh things about her. These are just public examples of the incivility that exists in our world, but the average person feels that same incivility every day.

Radio shock jocks use language on the air that would have cost them their jobs just a few years ago. The same is true of television. R-rated programming is the normal fare for television today. The on-air violence, sexuality, and language have desensitized many of us and have caused us to become less civil to one another. Many video games young people play and much of the music they listen to reinforce the idea that violence is the way to achieve what you want and that women exist merely for sexual pleasure.

News programs are not much different. Rarely can listeners hear two sides debate an issue because most discussions are nothing more than two people interrupting and yelling at each other. Journalists have adopted a philosophy of "if it bleeds, it leads," and they seem determined to make every issue as bloody as possible.[17] Exposure to a steady diet of that philosophy on the evening news has a negative impact on the civility of our society.

We've also raised a society of people who believe that the world truly does revolve around them and their needs. A mother recently asked me what she could do with her adult daughter who lacks any sense of responsibility. I told the mother that her daughter's world was very, very small. It consists only of her, and she only feels responsible for herself. It is her needs that must be met at all costs, and pity the person who would get between her and what she wants.

This same mind-set is played out through much of our population, and we see it in road rage, school shootings, frivolous lawsuits, and workplace rudeness.

My wife works in a retail store that sells fabric. She has had customers throw merchandise at her because they had to wait in line for her to cut their fabric. Customers have cursed and threatened her because the store did not carry some item they wanted. Virtually anyone who works in retail can tell similar stories.

Unfortunately, churches are not exactly the bastion of civility either. A pastor in our region was in jeopardy of losing his job. I worked with the governing board for several weeks to resolve the issues, of which the main one was a rather minor, but poor, decision on the part of the pastor for which he had apologized. It was decided he would be able to remain there as pastor. A few weeks later he returned from a denominational convention and was told that he should resign at the upcoming business meeting later that week and that if he did, the church would provide him with three months severance pay. He did announce his resignation that evening and was told after the meeting adjourned that the governing board had decided to only pay him for two months severance. He became just one more pastor terminated because of a mean-spirited faction in the church, and this, too, is a scenario that is being played out on almost a daily basis in our churches.

It is time we remember that all people are created in the image of God and deserve to be treated with respect and dignity. Even the people whose lifestyle choices you most disagree with are persons for whom Jesus Christ died, and whom He wishes to redeem to himself. Missional churches seek ways to reach out to people who have been hurt by the insensitivity and incivility of others.

Fear

There is much fear in our society today. Not long ago a student at Virginia Tech murdered 32 of his classmates. Violence is rampant in our culture, with reports of drive-by shootings and murders occurring in every major city. Even smaller communities are not immune. The small town in which I live was recently shocked when a young woman was murdered by people she considered her friends.

The fear people feel today is not limited to the violent behavior that threatens their well-being. People also fear losing their jobs as many companies continue to send their operations overseas to take advantage of the lower costs associated with doing business in many countries. In some cases, people have invested their lives in a company only to have it downsize and eliminate the positions for which they have been trained. Other companies file for bankruptcy and close, costing their employees not only their jobs but sometimes their pensions as well. One of the basic needs of human beings is security, and many people do not feel secure today; they are fearful of what the future may hold for them.

Many parents and grandparents worry about the world their children and grandchildren will grow up in. There is no question that future generations face dangers and threats that previous generations did not. Some couples are so fearful they have decided not to have children to avoid exposing them to these dangers.

MISSIONAL CHURCHES MUST MINISTER TO THE EXISTING CULTURE

In this chapter we have identified some of the common needs people have today. They need a community that is civil and respectful to one another and that provides a safe environment in which to live and raise future generations. That community should be found within our churches. The small, family church is uniquely positioned to be just that type of community.

Now that you know some of the general needs of people, you must next identify the specific needs within your community that your church could meet. However, once you identify those needs, you may wonder how the small church actually ministers to them. What has to happen in the small church for it to accomplish this task? What decisions must be made to enable a small church to move from a maintenance mind-set to a missional one? That will be the topic of the next chapter.

EIGHT

What Decisions Must Be Made?

The future is the sum total of all the choices that are made in the present and in the past.[1]

— Erwin Raphael McManus

Over the years your church has made many decisions that may not have seemed significant at the time, but every decision shapes us in some way. Your church is what it is today largely because of decisions it made in the past. Decisions that were made two decades earlier may continue to shape your church today. If your church is strong, healthy, and vital in its ministry to the community, congratulations! That means that good decisions were made in the past and that good decisions are probably still being made. However, if your church is stuck in a maintenance mode and is no longer making much of an impact on your community, then you need to take a serious look at the reasons for that. Most likely, it is because of poor decisions that were and are being made by the church.

Identifying the ministry needs in your community is only one part of becoming a missional church. The second part is deciding what you will do with that information.

Throughout this book I have asked the question, "Who are we here for?" You may identify many ministry needs in your community, but your church will still have to decide if it exists to meet those needs or if it exists to meet the needs of the existing members. Maintenance-minded congregations are convinced their church exists to meet the needs of the existing members. Few will admit that, but all one has to do is to look at their budget and their programs and it becomes clear that everything the church does is focused on maintaining the church and serving the current membership. Chances are that your church will look much different if it makes the decision to actively seek meaningful ways to reach out to its community.

I recently led a struggling church through a visioning process. One of the questions asked as we were drawing the day to a close was, "What would you like your church to look like in three years?" After hearing a few responses, I then asked, "What would have to change for those things to happen?"

Smaller churches cannot do everything. If they want to add new ministries that will target specific ministry needs, most of our churches will need to eliminate some of the other things they are doing. We do not have the resources—people, finances, time, and energy—to do everything. It is imperative that we identify the things we need to be doing and provide the resources to accomplish those things by eliminating the other things we are doing that are no longer productive.

We seem to forget that many of the activities currently done in most churches were begun to meet a need that was identified at that

> *To fail to set priorities means that everything will become a priority. When everything is a priority, then nothing is.*[2]
> —Aubrey Malphurs

time. Perhaps that need no longer exists, but we continue to offer that same ministry or program without evaluating its present effectiveness. If we want to be missional, we must identify the current needs we need to address, eliminate any ineffective ministries, and replace those ministries with new ones that will address the current needs.

THE DECISION TO GIVE PEOPLE TIME TO DO MINISTRY

Many of our smaller churches today continue to have a Sunday morning worship service, a Sunday evening service, and a midweek Bible study. I am not against worship services or Bible studies, but many smaller churches have found that the evening and midweek services are very poorly attended. People have so many demands on their lives today that most of them will not make time for the evening and midweek gatherings.

We complain about the poor turnout at these services and question people's commitment to God and to the church. Yet we also ask these people to sing in the choir, teach a class, and

> *Missional churches equip God's people to be on mission.*[3]
> —Milfred Minatrea

perhaps serve on two or three (or more) committees. Overwhelmed with all these maintenance activities, when will these people have the time to participate in the new missional vision of the church and lead new ministries designed to engage our community?

If we want our church members to become missionaries to our community, we will have to find ways to free up their time so they can actually do ministry. That may mean eliminating the evening and/ or midweek service. It may require eliminating those committees and boards that provide little or no real benefit to the church or community. It may mean that we entrust more decision making to our church leadership and not have a business meeting every time someone proposes changing a light bulb. If we do not find ways to free people up to do ministry, our churches will never become missional.

THE DECISION TO FIND THE BEST TIMES FOR WORSHIP SERVICES

Although this is changing a little, most of the churches in our area have their Sunday morning worship service starting at 10:30 or 11:00 and their evening service starting at 7:00. Most other meetings held at the church during the week are also held at 7:00, especially in the rural churches. For many years our association held a monthly men's meeting that started at 7:30. There is nothing wrong with any of these times, but how long has it been since your church discussed whether your worship and meeting times were the best times to meet?

These times were chosen when many in our area churches were farmers. At one time there were many dairy farms in our county, and in fact, I was raised on one. These times were set so the dairy farmers could milk their cows and still have time to make it to church. There are very few dairy farms in our county today. I asked that the monthly men's meeting start earlier, since none of the men had seen the business end of a cow for years, and two years later they did move their starting time to 7:00.

> *The center of any mission community's organized life is its corporate worship.*[4]
> —Darrell L. Guder

Are there people in your community that find your service times inconvenient? Many people today work on Sundays, often to feed the Christians who hurry to the restaurants after the church services end. When are these people supposed to have an opportunity to worship? Many churches are finding that starting a worship service on Saturday evening allows people to come to church who could not attend on Sunday morning. Others offer an earlier service starting at 8:00 or 8:30. One new church that recently opened in our community has its Sunday worship service at 2:00 in the afternoon. Judging from the cars in its parking lot, this church has several people that find that a convenient time.

THE DECISION ABOUT WORSHIP STYLES

Few things evoke more passion than discussing changing the style of worship in a church. Your present membership may find the current style of worship meaningful, but that style may not effectively impact the life of the target group your church believes God has called it to reach. Although music preferences often come to mind when people think about differences in style, style encompasses more than music. There are also differences in what people want from their worship experience. Many current members are satisfied with hearing songs and sermons about God. Those outside the church, especially those influenced by postmodernism, want to experience God.

T. S. Eliot used to tell the story of a person who walked past a baker's shop that had a sign advertising bread for a dollar a loaf. The man walked in the shop hungry for the bread and expecting to smell its hot, freshly baked aroma only to discover that the shop sold no bread, just copies of the sign advertising it. Eliot would conclude the story by saying the church was like that shop.[5] Many people today would agree with him. They need to experience God, not merely hear stories about Him, if He is to become real to them.

There are many ways to help people experience God. Music is one important way, but so is silence. Many of our church members become very uncomfortable during times of silence, but silence can be a powerful way to experience God. "Be still, and know that I am God" (Ps. 46:10).

Too often, the Lord's Supper is little more than an add-on at the end of our worship services. We go through the motions of sharing the bread and cup without really thinking about what we are experiencing. Seldom is the significance of what we are doing explained, yet this can be one of the most important times of the worship service. Rick Warren claims that they see more people come to Christ at Saddleback Church during the Communion service when it is fully explained than at any other service they have.[6]

I remember one Sunday when I became overwhelmed with the reality of the meaning of the Lord's Supper. As our deacons were taking the cup to the congregation, I began to think of what that cup represented to me. I was reminded of my sins that required the Lord to go to the Cross and give His life. I began to weep. I was able to control my emotions as I took the trays back from the deacons, but when I asked the congregation to drink the cup in remembrance of Christ, I began to weep again. It was one of the most powerful experiences of God that I have had in a worship service.

If postmodern worship can't make people furiously feel and think (in the modern world the church made people only "think"), it can't show them how God's Word transforms the way we "feel."[7]

—Leonard Sweet

Many churches are finding it helpful to use visuals during the worship service. Video projectors can be used to put the announcements on a screen before and after a service, and some ministers like to put sermon notes on the screen during the message, but the greatest use of visuals may be to create a richer worship experience. Images that draw people to God or to the theme of the service can enable worshippers to experience God in new ways.

Another way people can experience God in the worship service is by hearing the stories of how God is working in people's lives. We always had a time at Hebron when people could share with the rest of the congregation what God was doing in their lives. Many Sundays no one shared anything, but there were some services in which people had powerful testimonies to share. On a few Sundays these times of sharing were the most powerful part of the worship service. In larger churches it is difficult to provide a time during the worship service for people to tell how God is impacting their lives, but in smaller churches it is more easily done.

Preaching must also change in the missional church. When I began my pastoral ministry in 1981, it was sufficient to select a text and teach the congregation what the text meant. Nearly everyone in the congregation shared the same Christian worldview and understanding of God and the Bible. Not everyone in today's congregation shares those same beliefs, and they are not nearly as interested in what the text means as they are in learning what it might mean to them: "How will this message make a difference in my life and the things that I am dealing with?" Any time I prepare a new sermon I give it the "So what?" test. The

> *Preaching today must prove the Bible's relevancy, not presume it.*[8]   —Michael Hostetler

sermon may be biblically sound and theologically correct, but what difference is it likely to make in people's lives? Preaching to postmodern people requires the sermons to have practical application to their lives. This again shows the importance of understanding the culture and the target group you are trying to reach.

Clearly this demonstrates a problem that preachers face. If the church is seeking to become more missional and new people are attending the worship services, how does the preacher prepare sermons that will speak to both the existing membership and their guests? Seminary preaching professor Michael Quicke believes that "the twenty-first century desperately needs missional cross-cultural preaching that reaches the lost and energizes the found for witness and service."[9] I would recommend his book *360-Degree Preaching* to assist the preacher in this challenging responsibility.

We could not discuss worship styles without talking about music. I'm reluctant to even bring up the subject of music because of all the controversy that this topic generates, but if we are going to be missional we will have to address it. I know of a church that did a study of the most popular music stations in their community and found that the majority of people kept their radios tuned to a country music station. The music in their church reflects that preference. A cowboy church in a nearby community uses music with a Western sound to it. The church our daughter's family attends uses a lot of upbeat music with an urban sound. The thing each of these churches has in common is that their music reflects their target audience. These churches have decided that music is not going to be a barrier between them and the people they believe God has given them to reach.

This again brings up the question of how to provide a worship experience that will meet the needs of those four or five generations of people who may attend your service. Unless your church is a new church plant, you probably have some people who have attended services there for many years and who find the format of the service, the expository preaching style they are accustomed to, and the traditional hymns very meaningful. It would not be fair to them to suddenly change everything in order to be more appealing to a different target group.

> *The most biblical church is the one in which the cross is the only stumbling block for the unchurched.*[10]
>
> —Ed Stetzer

Some churches have been able to develop a very good blended worship service that at least offers different music styles in the service. In some churches this has worked well, but in others it does little to settle the debate on what appropriate worship should look like. I agree with Jill Hudson who doesn't believe most churches today can meet the worship needs of existing members and the people a church is trying to reach in only one worship service. She writes:

I am a strong proponent for all but the very newest of mainline congregations continuing to offer at least *one* weekly opportunity for worship based on the traditional forms. It would be unconscionable to discontinue forms of worship that have transported so many Christians to the presence of God over the years. I am equally committed to the position that all churches need to offer at least one alternative to that service to meet the highly diverse needs of a postmodern population.[11]

A maintenance-minded church will reject the idea of offering two or more worship services as soon as it is proposed. One of the arguments often heard is that we'll have two churches, and we won't know the people who attend the other service. My response is that may be true, but you don't know the people who don't attend any service either. Would you rather not know the people who attend the other worship service this church offers, or would you prefer that they continue to be separated from God because we don't want them to experience Him unless they do so exactly like we do?

The smaller, missional church may find the idea of having two worship services a little strange when the sanctuary could certainly hold many more people than now attend, but they are willing to do whatever it takes to reach people for Jesus Christ. This will allow worship services to be created that will meet the needs of both existing believers and those the church is seeking to reach. It takes a lot more work from the pastor and those who lead worship, but missional work is more challenging. It always has been, and we should not expect that to change in the twenty-first century.

DECIDING WHICH IS MORE IMPORTANT: BUILDINGS OR PEOPLE

Maintenance churches are easy to keep clean. Very little happens in them, and the people who attend know how to behave when they are "in church." On the other hand, missional churches can get messy. The carpet can get dirty because there are more people walking on it, and some of them don't know that they shouldn't spill a drink or track in mud from the outside. I've seen congregations excited about having small children in the church for the first time in years until they find sticky, little handprints on the walls and windows. About that time a self-appointed committee of concerned church members has a meeting with the parents, and those children suddenly disappear from the church along with their parents.

A small church built a beautiful new fellowship building believing it would enhance their outreach potential. The problem was that when the building was completed, the members didn't want anyone from the outside using the building. Church members asked to use the building to host groups and to offer some different ministries only to be refused. Other members didn't want to risk getting the carpets and walls dirty or having someone leave a mess in their new kitchen. Soon the church members requesting to use the building left that congregation. Instead of the new building being used as a tool to grow the church, it led the church to shrink in numbers.

Certainly, we should always want to keep our facilities clean and neat. They represent a significant investment, and it is a matter of good stewardship to protect that investment. On the other hand, churches need to make a decision about what is most important, their buildings or people. When I was pastor at Hebron, I would sometimes remind our rural congregation that our building would hold a lot of hay, and if we were not involved in the work of God, that might be all that building would be used for some day. Jesus gave His life for people, not for buildings and clean carpet. A dirty carpet can be cleaned, but a lost person who dies without Christ is lost forever. A missional church will see its building and property as simply one tool available to it to minister to the people that God cares about so much.

DECIDING IF WE REALLY LOVE PEOPLE

Perhaps this should have been our first question even before we started thinking about our worship services and buildings, because if we don't truly love people, we will not put them before other things. I'm sure that if we asked most people in our churches whether they were a loving congregation, they would insist that they were, but their attitudes and actions might tell another story.

We're losing the game not because we've forgotten what to say, but because we've forgotten how to love.[12]
—Tom Clegg and Warren Bird

A pastor moved into a new community and began developing relationships with people who were not members of his church. Four people in particular made an impression on him when they refused his invitation to receive Jesus Christ as their Savior. He invited each of these individuals to address his congregation during a four-week series of sermons to help the church understand why they were not reaching people with the gospel. The congregation heard from these people how they felt about Christians and the way Christians had treated them in the past. It was a painful time for the church, which lost a few people who became upset, but there was a genuine turnaround in the attitudes of the people who stayed.[13]

Unchurched people visit our churches and hear a lot of "us versus them" language. Such language automatically puts people on the defensive and creates immediate barriers that may well prevent future ministry opportunities.

Too often today's preaching can suggest an elitist mentality that the insiders of the church comprise the "good people" and those on the outside are the "bad people." To certain onlookers, the church's function can be mistaken as bringing in the "bad people" so that they can become "good people."[14]

Of course, one of the problems with this is when people, such as the four mentioned above, do not find that church people are necessarily good people. Many of them have seen the ways we treat one another and the way we treat others, and they do not want to become like that.

Jesus said, "By this all will know that you are My disciples, if you have love for one another" (John 13:35). Do we truly love one another? Does your church have a genuine love for those who are of a different culture or religious background? Does your church love those who hold to a very different worldview or live a different lifestyle? What will happen if a couple living together without benefit of marriage visits your church next Sunday? Will they be made to feel welcome? What if a group of Goth teenagers show up for your next youth gathering? What if the local drug pusher walks in at the start of your service? I'm not saying that the church should approve of sinful lifestyle choices—we shouldn't—but can your congregation see these people through the eyes of Jesus? Jesus

> *The church loves blue hair until it walks through its doors on a 16-year-old kid.*[15]
> —Leonard Sweet

sees each person as one for whom He died and wishes to redeem to himself—which is the same way He saw you and me when we were in sin and separated from Him.

Can your congregation offer a loving community to a person who is hurting because of the poor choices he or she has made in life? Can people who may feel like complete failures find unconditional love from the people in your church? A maintenance-minded church probably won't offer that kind of love because it is too risky to love someone like that. A missional church looks beyond the choices and appearances and seeks to love people to Jesus. It is willing to take the risk because it understands that this is its calling.

DECIDING TO TAKE THE RISK

Make no mistake, it is risky to move from a maintenance mindset to a missional one. Existing church members will have to sacrifice some of their preferences in order to reach out in a relevant way to people who may not initially share their values and beliefs. Some church members may decide to leave the congregation, and that does not mean they are bad people. The transformations the church may decide need to occur may not meet the needs those people have. Missional ministry can be expensive because the new people the church is reaching out to are unlikely to contribute much to the church, and the problem will be compounded if your tithers decide to leave the church. It will also be emotionally costly because the people you identify as your targeted group may be people with many social, financial, emotional, and spiritual needs requiring additional time from the pastor and congregational leaders.

God often calls us into risky situations. Jesus did not mince words when He explained to His disciples how they would suffer for His sake as they fulfilled their ministries after He was gone. In many parts of the world today Christians and churches experience constant dangers and challenges. It's risky for them to gather together or to own a Bible or to share their faith with others. For some reason, the church in North America seems to think that they have not been called to share in that risk.

Sometimes being in the will of God can be one of the scariest places you'll ever be in, but it's also the safest. When we are in the place where God wants us, He is able to do some great things in and through our lives. God has a mission for your church, and if you will join Him in that mission I believe you will be amazed at what you will see Him do.

It is even riskier to not make the change from being maintenance-minded to missional. Thom Rainer's research has found that "eight out of ten of the approximately 400,000 churches in the United States are declining or have plateaued."[16] A church does not stay on a plateau for very long before entering the decline stage. Citing Win Arn, Ed Stetzer reports that 80 to 85 percent of the churches in America have already entered the downside of their life cycle, and that thirty-five hundred to four thousand churches now close each year.[17]

One choice our churches must make is which risk we prefer taking. Would we rather risk the unknown and allow God to transform us so we can more effectively minister in this new age in which we find ourselves, or would we prefer risking the death of our church? Eventually, it really does come down to this choice. Unless our churches are able to start a new life cycle through new ministries, death is inevitable. Perhaps even sadder than the death of a church is the knowledge that many lives were not touched in any meaningful way by that church in the years before it closed its doors. The future of your church depends upon the decisions that are being made today. Your church will become what the congregation determines it will be by the choices they make now. What will your future look like?

NINE

The Future of the Small Church

God will be in this future, with or without us.[1]

—Leonard Sweet

What does the future hold for the smaller church? Some say that the smaller church can't survive much longer, that it will be swallowed up by the larger churches. I think it would be a mistake for anyone to write off the smaller church, because it has proven to be extremely hardy. For years now it has proven it can exist for a long time—even decades—on very little. Some churches will exist as long as there are enough resources to pay someone to come in and preach each Sunday and to pay the utility bills. Very little happens in this kind of church, but the people don't mind because they like their little church.

Other small churches will enjoy very productive ministries. They may never grow very large due to geographic or demographic reasons, but they attract people who prefer the small church setting to a larger church. These churches have identified clear ministry opportunities within their communities that also appeal to some people. These churches understand that God has placed them where they are for a specific purpose, they have discovered that purpose, and they are committed to living it out.

These two kinds of churches have very different futures, and those futures are largely determined by the choices these churches have made. This final chapter will examine what those futures might look like.

THE FUTURE OF THE MAINTENANCE CHURCH

The church in the first paragraph is the typical small maintenance church. Such churches have very low expectations and often don't achieve them. They talk a good talk about wanting to grow. They insist to their denominational leaders that they are committed to growth. Many in such a church remember the days when the church building was full and had a thriving youth ministry, and they are convinced that if they could resurrect that youth ministry, all would be right with the church again. Unfortunately, any attempt to reach out to the youth in the community, or anyone else, is opposed by those not wanting the church to make the changes required to reach new people.

They insist that their pastor be available to them 24-7. One such church chastised its pastor because he coached his son's little league baseball team. Members of the church told him that he had not been hired to coach a baseball team but to be their pastor. Another church had members critical of their pastor because he often performed funerals for people in the community who did not have a church home. He saw it as a ministry to families in a time of great need; the church members saw it as taking away time he could spend with them.

What is the future of the maintenance-minded church? It can expect to become grayer every year as its numbers decline. As the congregation ages and grows smaller, they will experience financial pressures as their giving dwindles. Routine maintenance on the facilities will not be done, making the facilities less attractive to those who might be searching for a church. Sunday School classes will be combined due to the decline in enrollment and the shortage of teachers. Combining classes will make them less appealing to families who might visit the church seeking a place to worship and serve.

These churches will find it increasingly more difficult to find and keep a pastor. Studies show that there is not a clergy shortage in America, but there are fewer ministers willing to serve in the smaller, declining churches.[2] Such churches may attract seminary student pastors or retired pastors, but neither of these is likely to remain at the church long enough to effect any significant turnaround. Some of these churches would do best if they find someone who has been called to bivocational ministry and can stay at the church long enough to change people's understanding of what it means to be a church.

One problem is that these churches often do not appreciate bivocational ministers. Longtime members remember when their pastors had advanced degrees and were among the most respected persons in the community. They are not willing now to settle for someone who works forty hours a week in the local factory while pastoring their church. A member of one declining church with an average attendance of around forty people called me one time asking if I would meet with their search committee, but before I could answer, the caller stated that she noted that I was a bivocational minister. She said I would have to leave my job if I went there as their pastor because they would never go backward by calling a bivocational minister. I asked why, if the church had only had full-time pastors for years, there were not more than forty people attending the church. I also informed her that any church that called me as their pastor would not be going backward even if I remained bivocational. Our conversation ended soon after that response!

These churches will also find that they will receive less assistance from their denominations. Denominations are experiencing the same financial problems that many churches face. As giving declines in the church, less money is being given to the denomination, which means less money is available for resource development and ministry assistance. Declining churches often look to their denominations for a program that will turn their situation around, but they are now finding that such programs do not exist. A wedge begins to form between the church and the denomination that may cause the church to leave the denomination because it doesn't believe it is getting any help anyway. The church may soon find that it is very lonely outside the denominational and associational relationships it has enjoyed over the years.

Members of the church talk more and more about how good it used to be there. Now, finances are down, attendance is down, there are few, if any, youth, they have had a succession of short-term pastors, and relations are strained between the church and their denomination. Is it any wonder that such churches often struggle with self-esteem issues? The members believe that their church is unattractive. They are no longer worthy of the support and leadership of a long-term pastor. The building is in poor shape, and there is no money to do the needed repairs. All they can do is preserve their resources and try to hold on while hoping for a miracle turnaround.

THE FUTURE OF THE MISSIONAL CHURCH

As we've seen throughout this book, the missional church is not interested in surviving but in ministering. This church understands that God has a much higher purpose for its continued existence than merely survival. There are people who need to touch God in order to have their lives forever transformed, and the missional church is seeking ways to help them do that. The missional church has the same limitations of every small church, but it sees its limited resources as the means to impact lives.

The missional church has narrowed down its ministry focus so that its resources can have the greatest impact. It understands it can't be all things to all people, so its congregation prayerfully seeks God's guidance for how they can best serve their community. This church understands that God is not redundant and does not expect every church to have the same exact ministry. Instead, He calls each church to a specific ministry that can be done with the financial resources and the spiritual gifts He has given it. The missional church is on mission with God. It has sought His vision for its preferred future, and it is committed to living out that future.

As a result, this church is enjoying a productive ministry in its community. The congregation has a singleness of purpose as many of the people have accepted ownership of a commonly understood vision. This results in fewer conflicts as there are fewer competing visions within the body. People are excited about being a part of a church that is having an impact on the community. Church leadership is entrusted to handle much of the administrative and maintenance tasks of the church, freeing up the membership to do ministry. Instead of spending another evening discussing the repair of a dripping kitchen faucet, church members are involved in fulfilling the vision God has for their church. And the faucet gets fixed just fine along the way!

People within the community see the ministry occurring through the life of this congregation, and some are attracted to it. They are looking for a way to make their lives count as well. Besides, they have some issues in their lives for which they would like some answers, and they find the people from this church are not afraid to talk about life's tough issues.

Because people give money to the causes they believe in, finances are less of a problem in the missional church. That does not mean there is an abundance of money, but there is always enough to maintain the facility, pay the bills, and support the vision. People are not giving to a faceless mission project being done somewhere else in the world; they are providing the funds to continue the work in their own community, and they are often the ones who are doing the work. Incidentally, I often find that missional churches not only give more money for their own local mission work but are also very supportive of their denomination's mission work.

Because of the ministry and the spirit that exists in these churches, they are able to attract and keep good pastors. Many of these pastors are also bivocational, but it is not uncommon to see these pastors remain at these church for ten years or longer. Due to their longer tenure they know the congregation and community better, and their messages reflect that knowledge. They are able to address biblically the issues that are confronting the people in the community. Unchurched persons seeking a church home appreciate the answers they hear from these pastors and the opportunity to develop relationships with these ministers outside the church setting.

THE CHOICE IS YOURS

Two very different futures, but they share one thing in common. Each future will come to pass because of the choices the congregation makes. If a church chooses to remain maintenance-minded, it can expect to see continued decline. Any church that puts most of its focus on itself is unlikely to experience much positive ministry or have any significant impact on its community. And eventually God will raise up another church in the community to reach the people who live there.

The church that commits itself to being missional will enjoy a productive and exciting ministry as it partners with God and His work in the community. Such a church may remain smaller in size due to the unique circumstances in which it finds itself, but it will not be small in heart or spirit, nor will it be small in its impact on the community.

Which future will your church choose for itself?

SWOT Analysis

Some businesses use a planning tool called a SWOT analysis that churches may find helpful as they attempt to identify potential ministry needs in their communities. SWOT stands for Strengths, Weaknesses, Opportunities, and Threats. Doing a SWOT analysis should be done by a team of leaders within the church. It is not a difficult exercise, but it is one that should not be rushed to ensure that a thorough analysis is performed. Let's look at how your church could use this tool.

STRENGTHS

What are the strengths of your church? Most leaders agree that it is best for any organization to work from its strengths, so it is vital for the church to identify its strengths. What gifts exist in your church? Each believer has been given at least one spiritual gift that is to be used in ministry (1 Cor. 12:1-11). Do the members of your church know what gifts they have? Do the leaders of your church know what spiritual gifts exist within the congregation? It has been my experience that many Christians do not know what their spiritual gifts are. There are tools that can help individuals and churches better understand what gifts the Holy Spirit has given them. If your congregation does not have a good understanding of the spiritual gifts that the people possess, it will be important to determine that before proceeding with the SWOT analysis. These spiritual gifts represent an important strength in your church. God will not give a church a vision for a ministry if that church does not have the ability to minister in that area of need.

Another component of a church's strengths is the passion of the people for a particular ministry. Some people have a passion for ministering to children, while others may have a passion for serving in a ministry to people in nursing homes. A third group of people may be passionate about serving in a soup kitchen and feeding the homeless. All three groups of people may share some common gifts, such as mercy, healing, and helps; but each of them are passionate about different ways to use those gifts. All three examples may be legitimate needs that exist in a community, and all three would be a good use of the gifts mentioned, but if no one in the congregation has a passion for one of these ministries, the church should not attempt to serve in that area.

As an example, let's say that there is a need for a ministry to feed the homeless in the community. No one really feels a passion for doing this, but because the need exists, some people volunteer to work in this area. What is likely to happen is that after a few weeks this ministry will become drudgery to those who have volunteered, and they will begin to find other things to do. Fewer and fewer people will show up each week for this ministry until it can no longer continue. The people who volunteered feel guilty about their lack of enthusiasm, the people who were being helped become disappointed with the church, and the church may revert back to its poor self-esteem and its maintenance mentality. After all, the failure of this ministry proves that this church cannot successfully minister to its community.

Remember, no one church can meet every ministry need that exists in a community. The ministry needs your church should attempt to meet are those for which it has gifted people who also have a passion about meeting those particular needs. When gifts and passion come together, it is a strength of the church.

WEAKNESSES

Some people believe that a church should focus on improving the areas where it is weak, but I disagree unless we are talking about a moral weakness. Working to improve a weakness will usually only lift that area of church life to average, while working to improve the areas that are already strong will make the church even stronger.

One of the strengths of the church I pastored for twenty years was hospitality. We were very good at making visitors feel comfortable and appreciated. I often joked that we did not have to make a special announcement in our worship service telling people to spend a few minutes greeting their neighbors and being nice to one another. It would be rare in our church if every visitor did not meet at least half our congregation either before the service or immediately afterward.

One area in which we were not strong was our church choir, primarily because they let me sing in it. Our choir practiced hard, and some songs we performed rather well, while others were an adventure to say the least. While our congregation appreciated our efforts, we were not going to build a ministry around our music program. We had a fine choir director who taught us much about music, but we were unlikely to ever become better than average no matter how much we practiced. Even if we had identified a ministry need around music, it would not have been a good ministry for us because that was not an area in which we were strong.

Some ministry needs should not be attempted because no one in the church has the ability to meet those needs. Some churches have started a parish nurse ministry, which can be a great ministry to existing members as well as to the community, but this is not a ministry to begin if no one in the congregation is a nurse or a nurse cannot be brought in to lead this ministry. Due to the growing number of people entering this country, some churches have identified teaching English as a second language as a ministry need, but if a church does not have someone with the ability to do that, it is probably not a good ministry for that church.

Every church has areas of strengths and weaknesses. There is no shame in identifying those areas of weaknesses and not building a ministry around them. In fact, it is good stewardship to build a ministry around the gifts and abilities that do exist in the church.

Strengths and weaknesses are discovered by looking inside the church. Looking to the community outside the church comes next as the leadership team examines the opportunities and threats that exist.

OPPORTUNITIES

What ministry opportunities exist in the community your church serves? The potential list is endless. Too many small churches only want to talk about starting a youth ministry to attract young people into the church, and they never look at other possible ministry opportunities that exist around them.

Unfortunately, Indiana has passed a law permitting legalized gambling on riverboats, and there are now several within an hour's drive of my house. I personally know people whose lives and marriages have been destroyed because of family members who became addicted to gambling. Churches in this area could look at starting a ministry for people with gambling addictions and for family members who suffer because of those addictions. Perhaps no one in the church would have the ability to lead that ministry, but could the church invite someone who has that training and provide a space where the ministry could meet?

Is there a need in your community for a ministry to people who have gone through a divorce? What about a ministry to widows and widowers? Is there a need for a ministry to women and their families who have lost a baby in a miscarriage? If the baby dies after being born, there is a funeral and people come and offer their condolences, but a family who loses their baby in a miscarriage usually do not receive the same support. Are there people in your community who have been hurt by prior experiences in a church and have turned their back on the church as a result? Although they may still love the Lord, they cannot trust the church. Can your church love them and offer them a safe place to worship and grow in their faith? How many families in your community homeschool their children? Is there a way you can partner with them to provide some resources? Is there a ministry your church can offer to single parents?

How many people in your community work on Sunday morning and would be willing to attend a worship service if it was held at some other time? Has anyone from your church approached these people to ask what time would be more convenient for them? Would a different worship format reach different people than you are currently reaching? What would that format look like? When would that service be offered?

Clearly we have not come close to exhausting the list of possible ministry opportunities. These are offered to start the reader thinking outside the box. There are ministry needs in every community besides starting a youth group. In fact, many churches in your community may already have a strong youth ministry, but there are many other ministry needs going unmet that your church may be able to meet. All it takes is going out into the community and asking questions and getting to know people.

THREATS

After you have made a list of ministry opportunities, your leadership team must determine the threats that exist that will make it difficult for your church to meet these opportunities. We've already identified some of the threats. For instance, if your church does not have people with the ability or passion to minister in a certain area of need, your church probably should not try to minister to that need. Let another church in the community minister in that area.

Here's another possible threat: if you have identified a ministry need but find that another church has already developed a strong ministry in that area, you may not want to compete with that. For example, your SWOT analysis may have identified a large number of young people in your community, but then you find that the community church down the street already has a strong youth ministry with a full-time staff person serving two hundred young people through their multipurpose family life center and their strong Upward Bound sports program. You also learn that new young people attend their gatherings almost every week. Why would your church of 40 people want to compete with that? It is unlikely you would be able to develop a strong youth ministry that would be better than what the other church is already doing. That would be a threat to your success in that ministry. You would be better off focusing your ministry efforts toward some need other churches are not meeting.

The SWOT analysis can be a helpful tool to determine the ministry opportunities that might exist for your church. When used with the other visioning tools mentioned earlier in the book, it can lead a missional church into an exciting time of ministry to the community God has given it to serve.

NOTES

CHAPTER 1

1. J. Andrew Kirk, *What Is Mission? Theological Explorations* (Minneapolis: Fortress Press, 2000), 30.

2. George R. Hunsberger, *Missional Church: A Vision for the Sending of the Church in North America,* ed. Darrell L. Guder (Grand Rapids: William B. Eerdmans Publishing Co., 1998), 82.

3. Milfred Minatrea, *Shaped by God's Heart: The Passion and Practices of Missional Churches* (San Francisco: Jossey-Bass, 2004), 92.

4. Michael J. Quicke, *360-Degree Preaching: Hearing, Speaking, and Living the Word* (Grand Rapids: Baker Academic, 2003), 71.

5. Rick Warren, *The Purpose-Driven Church: Growth Without Compromising Your Message and Mission* (Grand Rapids: Zondervan, 1995), 169.

6. Lee Stroebel, *Inside the Mind of Unchurched Harry and Mary* (Grand Rapids: Zondervan, 1993), 13.

7. Darrell L. Guder and Lois Barrett, eds., *Missional Church: A Vision for the Sending of the Church in North America* (Grand Rapids: William B. Eerdmans Publishing Co., 1998), 5.

8. Thomas G. Bandy, *Fragile Hope: Your Church in 2020* (Nashville: Abingdon Press, 2002), 29-40.

9. Minatrea, *Shaped by God's Heart,* 30.

10. Paul D. Borden, *Hit the Bullseye: How Denominations Can Aim the Congregation at the Mission Field* (Nashville: Abingdon Press, 2003), 21.

11. Klyne Snodgrass, *The NIV Application Commentary: Ephesians* (Grand Rapids: Zondervan Publishing House, 1996), 224.

12. Mike Regele, *Death of the Church* (Grand Rapids: Zondervan, 1995), 222.

13. Thomas G. Bandy, *Kicking Habits: Welcome Relief for Addicted Churches* (Nashville: Abingdon Press, 2001), 138.

14. John Maxwell, *Failing Forward: Turning Mistakes into Stepping Stones for Success* (Nashville: Thomas Nelson, 2000), 124.

15. Minatrea, *Shaped by God's Heart,* 159.

16. Andy Stanley, *The Next Generation Leader: 5 Essentials for Those Who Will Shape the Future* (Sisters, Oreg.: Multnomah Publishers, 2003), 45.

17. Ed Stetzer and David Putman, *Breaking the Missional Code: Your Church Can Become a Missionary in Your Community* (Nashville: Broadman and Holman, 2006), 44.

CHAPTER 2

1. Quoted in Regele, *Death of the Church*, 52.

2. Dennis Bickers, *The Healthy Small Church: Diagnosis and Treatment for the Big Issues* (Kansas City: Beacon Hill Press of Kansas City, 2005), 20.

3. Loren Mead, *The Once and Future Church: Reinventing the Congregation for a New Mission Frontier* (Herndon, Va.: Alban Institute, 1991), 70.

4. Leonard Sweet, *Carpe Mañana* (Grand Rapids: Zondervan, 2001), 88.

5. "Americans 'Need' Their Gadgets," *Wired Magazine*, http://www.wired.com/news/technology/1,69896-0.html (accessed December 23, 2005).

6. Timothy JohnPress, "Staying Ahead of Change Requires Perspective," *Austin Business Journal*, September 6, 2004, http://www.austin.bizjournals.com/Austin/stories/2004/09/06/smallb2.html (accessed December 20, 2005).

7. Sweet, *Carpe Mañana*, 92.

8. Quoted in Leonard Sweet, *SoulSalsa* (Grand Rapids: Zondervan, 2000), 65.

9. Sweet, *Carpe Mañana*, 93.

10. Ibid., 33.

11. "Internet Usage Statistics for the Americas," *Internet World Stats*, http://www.internetworldstats.com/stats2.htm (accessed December 21, 2005).

12. John Dart, "Connected Congregations," *Christian Century* (February 7, 2001).

13. George Barna, "New Research Describes Use of Technology in Churches," *The Barna Update*, April 28, 2008, http://www.barna.org/FlexPage.aspx?Page=BarnaUpdateNarrow&BarnaUpdateID=297 (accessed October 17, 2008).

14. U.S. Census Bureau, 2004, "U.S. Interim Projections by Age, Sex, Race, and Hispanic Origin," http://www.census.gov/ipc/www/usinterimproj (accessed December 27, 2005).

15. Thomas L. Friedman, *The World Is Flat: A Brief History of the Twenty-First Century* (New York: Farrar, Straus, and Giroux, 2005), 40-41.

16. George Barna and Mark Hatch, *Boiling Point: It Only Takes One Degree* (Ventura, Calif.: Regal, 2001), 78.

17. Ibid., 84-85.

18. Thom S. Rainer, *Surprising Insights from the Unchurched* (Grand Rapids: Zondervan, 2001), 45.

19. Colleen Carroll, *The New Faithful: Why Young Adults Are Embracing Christian Orthodoxy* (Chicago: Loyola Press, 2002), 7.

20. Donald E. Miller, *Reinventing American Protestantism* (Berkley, Calif.: University of California Press, 1997), 28-29.

21. Leonard Sweet, *Post-Modern Pilgrims: First Century Passion for the 21st Century World* (Nashville: Broadman and Holman, 2000), 43.

22. Brian D. McLaren, *The Church on the Other Side: Doing Ministry in the Postmodern Matrix* (Grand Rapids: Zondervan, 2000), 183.

23. Warren, *Purpose-Driven Church*, 280-81.

24. Ibid., 282.

25. Bickers, *Healthy Small Church*, 36.

26. Reggie McNeal, *The Present Future: Six Tough Questions for the Church* (San Francisco: Jossey-Bass, 2003), 15.

CHAPTER 3

1. Alan J. Roxburgh, "Missional Leadership: Equipping God's People for Mission," *Missional Church: A Vision for the Sending of the Church in North America,* ed. Darrell L. Guder (Grand Rapids: William B. Eerdmans Publishing Co., 1998), 183.

2. Ronald A. Heifetz and Marty Linsky, *Leadership on the Line: Staying Alive Through the Dangers of Leading* (Boston: Harvard Business School Press, 2002), 13.

3. Maxwell, *Failing Forward,* 115.

4. Ibid., 216.

5. Aubrey Malphurs, *Advanced Strategic Planning: A New Model for Church and Ministry Leaders* (Grand Rapids: Baker Books, 1999), 44.

6. Leith Anderson, *A Church for the 21st Century* (Minneapolis: Bethany House Publishers, 1992), 46.

7. Anthony Pappas, "The Need for Spiritual Passion," A response to Adair T. Lummis, "What Do Lay People Want in Pastors?" Pulpit and Pew Research Reports, Duke Divinity School, 2003, http://www.pulpitandpew.duke.edu/PastorSearch.pdf (accessed June 10, 2006).

8. John C. Maxwell, *The 17 Indisputable Laws of Teamwork: Embrace Them and Empower Your Team* (Nashville: Thomas Nelson, 2001), 8.

9. http://www.belmont.edu/moench.

10. Alan J. Roxburgh and Fred Romanuk, *The Missional Leader: Equipping Your Church to Reach a Changing World* (San Francisco: Jossey-Bass, 2006), 134.

11. Ron Crandall, *Turnaround Strategies for the Small Church,* Effective Church Series, ed. Herb Miller (Nashville: Abingdon Press, 1995), 32.

12. Bill Easum, *Put On Your Own Oxygen Mask First: Rediscovering Ministry* (Nashville: Abingdon Press, 2004), 29.

13. James M. Kouzes and Barry Z. Posner, *Christian Reflections on the Leadership Challenge* (San Francisco: Jossey-Bass, 2004), 122.

14. George Barna, *The Power of Team Leadership: Finding Strength in Shared Responsibility* (Colorado Springs, Colo.: WaterBrook Press, 2001), 17.

15. Roxburgh, *Missional Church,* 214.

16. N. Graham Standish, *Becoming a Blessed Church: Forming a Church of Spiritual Purpose, Presence, and Power* (Bethesda, Md.: Alban Institute, 2005), 144.

17. Ibid., 130.

18. C. H. Spurgeon, *Lectures to My Students* (London: Passmore and Alabaster, 1875), 4, 3.

19. Standish, *Becoming a Blessed Church,* 131.

20. Crandall, *Turnaround Strategies for the Small Church,* 42.

21. Warren Bennis, *On Becoming a Leader* (Cambridge, Mass.: Perseus Publishing, 2003), 91.

22. Minatrea, *Shaped by God's Heart,* 159.

23. Bill Easum, "Risks Required in Turnaround Churches," *Taking Risks in Ministry,* ed. Dale Calloway (Kansas City: Beacon Hill Press of Kansas City, 2003), 102.

24. Regele, *Death of the Church,* 95.

25. Crandall, *Turnaround Strategies for the Small Church,* 69.

26. Henry Blackaby and Richard Blackaby, *Spiritual Leadership: Moving People on to God's Agenda* (Nashville: Broadman and Holman, 2001), 83.

27. Warren, *Purpose-Driven Church*, 111.

28. Max DePree, *Leadership Jazz* (New York: Dell Publishing, 1992), 100.

29. Glenn Daman, *Shepherding the Small Church: A Leadership Guide for the Majority of Today's Churches* (Grand Rapids: Kregel, 2002), 237.

30. John P. Kotter, *Leading Change* (Boston: Harvard Business School Press, 1996), 93.

31. Daman, *Shepherding the Small Church*, 238.

32. Elena Larsen, "Wired Churches; Wired Temples," Pew Internet and American Life Project, December 20, 2000, http://www.pewinternet.org/pdfs/PIP_Religion_Report.pdf (accessed December 29, 2006), 2.

33. "Churches aren't making full use of the power of the Internet," Ellison Research, January 6, 2006, http://www.ellisonresearch.com/releases/20060108.htm (accessed December 29, 2006).

34. American Bible Society: For Ministry [Internet]: available from http://www.forministry.com (accessed January 2, 2007).

35. Blogger [Internet]; available from http://www.blogger.com (accessed January 6, 2007).

36. Easum, *Put On Your Own Oxygen Mask First*, 104.

37. Marcus Buckingham and Donald O. Clifton, *Now, Discover Your Strengths* (New York: Free Press, 2001), 27.

38. Standish, *Becoming a Blessed Church*, 135.

39. Crandall, *Turnaround Strategies for the Small Church*, 37.

40. Quoted in Quicke, *360-Degree Preaching*, 95.

41. Jim Herrington, R. Robert Creech, and Trisha Taylor, *The Leader's Journey: Accepting the Call to Personal and Congregational Transformation* (San Francisco: Jossey-Bass, 2003), 12.

42. Eugene H. Peterson, *The Contemplative Pastor: Returning to the Art of Spiritual Direction* (Grand Rapids: William B. Eerdmans Publishing Co., 1989), 19.

43. Irvin A. Busenitz, "Training for Pastoral Ministry," *Rediscovering Pastoral Ministry*, ed. John MacArthur Jr. (Dallas: Word Publishing, 1995), 119.

44. John C. Maxwell, *The 21 Irrefutable Laws of Leadership: Follow Them and People Will Follow You* (Nashville: Thomas Nelson Publishers, 1998), 143.

CHAPTER 4

1. Jack Welch, *Winning* (New York: HarperCollins, 2005), 134.

2. Anthony B. Robinson, "This Thing Called Church," *Alban Congregational Magazine*, Winter 2006, http://www.alban.org/ShowArticle.asp?ID=311&Current=y (accessed January 16, 2006).

3. Sweet, *Carpe Mañana*, 153.

4. Referred to in Richard Southern and Robert Norton, *Cracking Your Congregation's Code* (San Francisco: Jossey-Bass, 2001), 8.

5. Jeffrey D. Jones, *Traveling Together: A Guide for Disciple-Forming Congregations* (Herndon, Va.: Alban Institute, 2006), 17.

6. Quoted in Robinson, "This Thing Called Church."

7. Rainer, *Surprising Insights from the Unchurched*, 127.

8. Carroll, *New Faithful*, 117.

9. Minatrea, *Shaped by God's Heart*, 104.

10. Malphurs, *Advanced Strategic Planning*, 52-53.

11. Thomas G. Bandy, *Moving Off the Map: A Field Guide to Changing the Congregation* (Nashville: Abingdon Press, 1998), 147-52.

12. Ibid., 163.

13. Ibid., 166-70.

14. Malphurs, *Advanced Strategic Planning*, 135.

15. George Barna, *The Power of Vision* (Ventura, Calif.: Regal Books, 1992), 28.

16. Bickers, *Healthy Small Church*, 101-2.

17. Leonard Sweet, *The Gospel According to Starbucks: Living with a Grande Passion* (Colorado Springs, Colo.: WaterBrook Press, 2007), 61.

18. Thom S. Rainer, *Breakout Churches: Discover How to Make the Leap* (Grand Rapids: Zondervan, 2005), 105.

19. Barna, *Power of Vision*, 110.

20. David McAlister-Wilson, "Reflections on Inspire a Shared Vision," *Christian Reflections on the Leadership Challenge*, eds. James M. Kouzes and Barry Z. Posner (San Francisco: Jossey-Bass, 2004), 56.

21. Robert Nash Jr., *An 8-Track Church in a CD World: The Modern Church in the Postmodern World* (Macon, Ga.: Smyth and Helwys Publishing, 1997), 102.

CHAPTER 5

1. Lyle Schaller, *Strategies for Change* (Nashville: Abingdon Press, 1993), 10.

2. D. Michael Abrashoff, *It's Your Ship* (New York: Warner Books, 2002), 15.

3. Minatrea, *Shaped by God's Heart*, xviii.

4. Malphurs, *Advanced Strategic Planning*, 39.

5. Ibid., 42.

6. Ibid., 46.

7. Ibid., 50.

8. Mead, *Once and Future Church*, 62.

9. Malphurs, *Advanced Strategic Planning*, 48-49.

10. Thom Rainer, "Top 10 Predictions for the Church by 2010," Church Central. Com, http://churchcentral.com/nw/s/template/Article.html/id/17796 (accessed December 23, 2005).

11. Dennis W. Bickers, *The Bivocational Pastor* (Kansas City: Beacon Hill Press of Kansas City, 2004), chap. 6.

12. Clay Smith, "Ten Ways to Build a Healthier Congregation," *Inside the Small Church*, ed. Tony Pappas (Herndon, Va.: Alban Institute, 2002), 59.

13. Gilbert R. Rendle, *Leading Change in the Congregation* (Herndon, Va.: Alban Institute, 1998), 64.

14. Dennis W. Bickers, *The Tentmaking Pastor: The Joy of Bivocational Ministry* (Grand Rapids: Baker Books, 2000).

15. H. B. London Jr. and Neil B. Wiseman, *The Heart of a Great Pastor: How to Grow Strong and Thrive Wherever God Has Planted You* (Ventura, Calif.: Regal, 1994), 26.

16. Ibid., 20.

17. Lynn Hybels and Bill Hybels, *Rediscovering Church: The Story and Vision of Willow Creek Community Church* (Grand Rapids: Zondervan, 1995), 187.

18. Douglas Groothuis, *Truth Decay: Defending Christianity Against the Challenges of Postmodernism* (Downers Grove, Ill.: InterVarsity Press, 2000), 69.

19. Sweet, *Gospel According to Starbucks*, 30.

20. Quoted as a popular saying in Patrick Morley, *Effective Men's Ministry* (Grand Rapids: Zondervan, 2001), 10.

21. Rendle, *Leading Change in the Congregation,* 59.

22. Ibid., 58.

23. Bickers, *Healthy Small Church.*

24. Bandy, *Moving Off the Map,* 115.

25. Malcolm Gladwell, *The Tipping Point: How Little Things Can Make a Big Difference* (Boston: Little, Brown, and Co., 2002), 255-56.

26. Peter M. Senge, *The Fifth Discipline: The Art and Practice of the Learning Organization* (New York: Currency Doubleday, 1990), 95.

27. George Barna, "Most Churches Did Not Answer the Phone," *The Barna Update,* January 26, 2004, http://www.barna.org/FlexPage.aspx?Page=BarnaUpdate &BarnaUpdateID=157 (accessed February 16, 2006).

CHAPTER 6

1. Kenneth O. Gangel, *Team Leadership in Christian Ministry* (Rev. ed.; Chicago: Moody Press, 1997), 212.

2. This story was first told in Bickers, *Healthy Small Church,* 53.

3. Chris Turner, "More than 1,300 Staff Dismissed in 2005: Relationship Issues Again Take First Five Spots," *LifeWay,* October 2, 2006, http://www.lifeway.com/lwc/article_main_page/0%2C1703%2CA%25253D163808%252 (accessed November 14, 2006).

4. Schaller, *Strategies for Change,* 42-43.

5. Max DePree, *Leadership Is an Art* (New York: Bantam Dell, 1989), 11.

6. Kotter, *Leading Change,* 21.

7. Doug Murren, "The Leader as Change Agent," *Leaders on Leadership,* ed. George Barna (Ventura, Calif.: Regal, 1997), 205.

8. Jim Herrington, Mike Bonem, and James H. Furr, *Leading Congregational Change: A Practical Guide for the Transformational Journey* (San Francisco: Jossey-Bass, 2000), 35.

9. Kotter, *Leading Change,* 42.

10. Bandy, *Kicking Habits,* 189.

11. Heifetz and Linsky, *Leadership on the Line,* 110.

12. Crandall, *Turnaround Strategies for the Small Church,* 37.

13. Schaller, *Strategies for Change,* 30.

14. Hans Finzel, *Change Is like a Slinky: 30 Strategies for Promoting and Surviving Change in Your Organization* (Chicago: Northfield Publishing, 2004), 141.

15. Herb Miller, *The Parish Paper* 9, no. 9 (Lubbock, Tex., March 2002).

16. Jeff Woods, "New Tasks for the New Congregation: Reflections on Congregational Studies," *Resources for American Christianity,* http://www.resourcingchristianity.org/downloads/essays/J%Woods%20Essay.pdf (accessed January 11, 2006).

17. Heifetz and Linsky, *Leadership on the Line,* 11.

18. Bandy, *Fragile Hope,* 126.

19. Ibid., 29.

20. Ibid., 129.

21. Minatrea, *Shaped by God's Heart,* 89.

22. Rainer, *Breakout Churches,* 196.

23. George Barna, *Revolution* (Wheaton, Ill.: Tyndale House, 2005), 91.

24. Kotter, *Leading Change,* 11.

25. Jill M. Hudson, *When Better Isn't Enough: Evaluation Tools for the 21st-Century Church* (Herndon, Va.: Alban Institute, 2004), 16-17.

CHAPTER 7

1. Craig Van Gelder, *Missional Church: A Vision for the Sending of the Church in North America,* ed. Darrell L. Guder (Grand Rapids: William B. Eerdmans Publishing Co., 1998), 18.

2. "Sexually Suggestive Sermons from Michigan Pastor Leave Some Hot and Bothered," Fox News, February 26, 2007, http://www.foxnews.com/printer_friendly_story/0,3566,254684,00.html (accessed February 27, 2007).

3. John MacArthur, "Grunge Christianity and Cussing Pastors? What Next?" *Military Ministry,* http://www.crosswalk.com/pastors/11530376 (accessed February 27, 2007).

4. Lois Barrett, *Missional Church: A Vision for the Sending of the Church in North America,* ed. Darrell L. Guder (Grand Rapids: William B. Eerdmans Publishing Co., 1998), 128.

5. Ibid., 114.

6. Doug Murren, *The Baby Boomerang: Catching Baby Boomers as They Return to Church* (Ventura, Calif.: Regal Books, 1990), 35.

7. Erin Curry, "Barna: Young Pastors Form New Portrait of Church Leadership," *Baptist Press,* February 19, 2004, http://www.bpnews.net/bpnews.asp?Id=17683 (accessed March 26, 2007).

8. Thom S. Rainer, *The Bridger Generation* (Nashville: Broadman and Holman Publishers, 1997), 64.

9. Randy Frazee, *The Connecting Church: Beyond Small Groups to Authentic Community* (Grand Rapids: Zondervan, 2001), 43.

10. Robert D. Putnam, *Bowling Alone: The Collapse and Revival of American Community* (New York: Simon and Schuster, 2000), 60.

11. Ibid., 98.

12. Ibid., 112.

13. Noted in Frazee, *Connecting Church,* 24.

14. Joseph A. Michelli, *The Starbucks Experience: 5 Principles for Turning Ordinary into Extraordinary* (New York: McGraw-Hill, 2007), 22.

15. Howard Schultz, *Pour Your Heart into It: How Starbucks Built a Company One Cup at a Time* (New York: Hyperion, 1997), 250.

16. Israel Galindo, *The Hidden Lives of Congregations: Understanding Church Dynamics* (Herndon, Va.: Alban Institute, 2004), 28.

17. Robert C. L. Moffat, "Incivility as a Barometer of Societal Decay," *Florida Philosophical Review,* Vol. 1, Issue 1, Summer 2001, http://www.cah.ucf.edu/philosophy.fpr/journals/volume1/issue1/Moffat.html (accessed June 2, 2007).

CHAPTER 8

1. Erwin Raphael McManus, *Uprising: A Revolution of the Soul* (Nashville: Thomas Nelson, 2003), 237.

2. Malphurs, *Advanced Strategic Planning,* 179.

3. Minatrea, *Shaped by God's Heart,* 25.

4. Guder, *Missional Church,* 241.

5. Sweet, *Gospel According to Starbucks,* 50.

6. Dan Kimball, *The Emerging Church: Vintage Christianity for All New Generations* (Grand Rapids: Zondervan, 2003), 164.

7. Sweet, *Post-Modern Pilgrims,* 43.

8. Michael Hostetler, *Introducing the Sermon: The Art of Compelling Beginnings* (Grand Rapids: Zondervan, 1986), 24.

9. Quicke, *360-Degree Preaching,* 136.

10. Ed Stetzer, *Planting Missional Churches* (Nashville: Broadman and Holman, 2006), 42.

11. Hudson, *When Better Isn't Enough,* 65.

12. Tom Clegg and Warren Bird, *Lost in America: How You and Your Church Can Impact the World Next Door* (Loveland, Colo.: Group Publishing, 2001), 127.

13. Ibid., 127-29.

14. Graham Johnston, *Preaching to a Postmodern World: A Guide to Reaching Twenty-First Century Listeners* (Grand Rapids: Baker Books, 2001), 127.

15. Sweet, *Carpe Mañana,* 27.

16. Rainer, *Breakout Churches,* 45.

17. Stetzer, *Planting Missional Churches,* 13.

CHAPTER 9

1. Sweet, *Carpe Mañana,* 27.

2. Patricia M. Y. Chang, "Assessing the Clergy Supply in the 21st Century," *Pulpit & Pew Research Reports,* Duke Divinity School, 2004, http://www.pulpitand-pew.duke.edu/chang.html (accessed June 10, 2006).